P9-CEN-457

# GRAMMAR SMART

## 3rd Edition

**The Staff of the Princeton Review**

princetonreview.com

PENGUIN RANDOM HOUSE

The Princeton Review
24 Prime Parkway, Suite 201
Natick, MA 01760
E-mail: editorialsupport@review.com

Published in the United States by
Random House LLC, New York, and
simultaneously in Canada by Random
House of Canada Limited, Toronto.
A Penguin Random House Company.

ISBN 978-0-8041-2590-1
ISSN 2372-7195

Editor: Calvin Cato
Production Editor: Beth Hanson
Production Artist: Gabriel Berlin

Printed in the United States of America
on partially recycled paper.

10 9 8 7 6 5 4 3 2 1

Third Edition

## Editorial

Rob Franek, Senior VP, Publisher
Casey Cornelius, VP Content Development
Mary Beth Garrick, Director of Production
Selena Coppock, Managing Editor
Calvin Cato, Editor
Colleen Day, Editor
Aaron Riccio, Editor
Meave Shelton, Editor
Orion McBean, Editorial Assistant

## Random House Publishing Team

Tom Russell, Publisher
Alison Stoltzfus, Publishing Manager
Melinda Ackell, Associate Managing Editor
Ellen Reed, Production Manager
Kristin Lindner, Production Supervisor
Andrea Lau, Designer

# Acknowledgments

For their sparkling grammatical know-how and generally inspirational presences, The Princeton Review would like to thank Marcia Lerner, Jennifer Grant, Tereze Glück, Lisa Cornelio, Thomas Glass, Stuart Mickle, Julian Fleisher, Laurice Pearson, and Betsy Goldstein.

The Princeton Review would also like to give special thanks to David Stoll for his hard work in updating the current edition of *Grammar Smart*.

# Contents

# Introduction

# How Important Is Grammar, Really?

Because you are reading these words, we assume you already believe grammar is important. In fact, it is the bedrock of clear communication. While you may communicate informally with friends or family (we do!), when it comes to the academic and professional realm, writing well and speaking well require the proper use of grammar. The rules of grammar exist to ensure clarity, and proper use of grammar shows you care about effective communication. It is awesome that you are interested in learning more about how to *own* English language grammar, as doing so will give you an incredible tool that you can use throughout your life.

- The proper use of grammar will lead to better grades on essays in high school and college.

- Grammar is tested on both major college entrance exams, the SAT and the ACT.

- Your college application essays need to be grammatically perfect.

- If you want to go to business school, grammar is tested on the business school entrance exam, the GMAT.

- You will rely on your knowledge of grammar in any job that requires you to write—and most professional jobs do!

Let's take a look at how grammar serves to clarify what could be ambiguous. For each sentence, write what the sentence actually means (which may be different from what it is trying to say), and then try to correct the sentence.

*Let's eat grandpa!*

Means: _____

Corrected: _____

*Toilet only for disabled elderly pregnant children.*

Means: _____

Corrected: _____

The Hunger Games *star Josh Hutcherson has a new home as well as a new nose which used to be owned by the late Heath Ledger.*

Means: _____

Corrected: _____

*Employees must wash all their hands prior to returning to work.*

Means: _____

Corrected: _____

*Eaten for good health, people enjoy fresh fruit for its sweet taste.*

Means: _____

Corrected: _____

And a tricky one:

*We invited the strippers, Katy Perry and Jay-Z.*

Means: _____

Corrected: _____

Turn to page 11 to see if you got them all right! For any that you missed, you'll find out why the corrected versions are required as you read the book.

# Getting Started: Your Knowledge, Your Expectations

Your route to mastery of grammar depends a lot on how you plan to use this book. Making your game plan starts with knowing where you are, and where you want to go.

First, let's establish why you are using this book.

My goal is to

1. become a grammar rock star; I want to know it all.
2. master the grammar tested on the SAT.
3. master the grammar tested on the ACT.
4. master the grammar on the GMAT.

Based on your answer above, respond to the following questions.

| Goal Number | Question |
|---|---|
| 1, 2, 3, 4 | How comfortable are you with the names of *Parts of Speech?*<br>(A) Completely, down to reflexive pronouns<br>(B) I know the basics, such as nouns and verbs<br>(C) Uh, what? |
| 1, 2, 3, 4 | How comfortable are you with the *Elements of Sentences?*<br>(A) Completely, down to predicates<br>(B) I know the basics, such as subjects and objects<br>(C) Uh, what? |

| Goal Number | Question |
|---|---|
| 1, 2, 3, 4 | How comfortable are you with *Subject-Verb Agreement?*<br>(A) Completely, down to collective nouns<br>(B) I know the basics, such as ignoring irrelevant prepositional phrases<br>(C) Uh, what? |
| 1, 2, 3, 4 | How comfortable are you with *Pronoun-Noun Agreement?*<br>(A) Completely, down to collective pronouns<br>(B) I know the basics, such as he versus him<br>(C) Uh, what? |
| 1, 2, 3, 4 | How comfortable are you with *Parallel Construction?*<br>(A) Completely, down to either...or<br>(B) I know the basics, such as lists<br>(C) Uh, what? |
| 1, 2, 4 | How comfortable are you with *Misplaced Modifiers?*<br>(A) Completely, down to a modifier at the end of a sentence<br>(B) I know the basics, such as a modifier at the beginning of a sentence<br>(C) Uh, what? |
| 1, 2, 4 | How comfortable are you with *Comparison Flaws?*<br>(A) Completely, down to when to use that or those<br>(B) I know the basics, such as noticing missing apostrophes<br>(C) Uh, what? |

| Goal Number | Question |
|---|---|
| 1, 2, 3, 4 | How comfortable are you with *Idioms*?<br>(A) Completely, down to fall off (not off of) the bed<br>(B) I know the basics, such as try to (not and)<br>(C) Uh, what? |
| 1 | How comfortable are you with *Diction*?<br>(A) Completely, down to indifferent versus disinterested<br>(B) I know the basics, such as can versus may<br>(C) Uh, what? |
| 1, 2, 4 | How comfortable are you with *Redundancy*?<br>(A) Completely, down to reason and because<br>(B) I know the basics, such as small in size<br>(C) Uh, what? |
| 1, 2, 3, 4 | How comfortable are you with *Commas*?<br>(A) Completely, down to appositives<br>(B) I know the basics, such as introductory clauses<br>(C) Uh, what? |
| 1 | How comfortable are you with *Periods versus Semicolons*?<br>(A) Completely, down to when to use semicolons in a list<br>(B) I know the basics, such as the similarity between the two<br>(C) Uh, what? |

| Goal Number | Question |
|---|---|
| 1, 3 | How comfortable are you with *Colons*?<br>(A) Completely, down to the need for a complete idea before the colon<br>(B) I know the basics, such as using a colon before a list<br>(C) Uh, what? |
| 1, 3 | How comfortable are you with *Dashes*?<br>(A) Completely, down to its role as a colon<br>(B) I know the basics, such as using them to set off an aside<br>(C) Uh, what? |
| 1, 3 | How comfortable are you with *Apostrophes*?<br>(A) Completely, down to their use in pronouns<br>(B) I know the basics, such as when to use them with nouns<br>(C) Uh, what? |
| 1 | How comfortable are you with *Parentheses, Hyphens, Question Marks, Quotation Marks, Voice, and Mood*?<br>(A) Completely<br>(B) Partially<br>(C) Uh what? |

# Your Guide To Getting The Most Out Of This Book

This book is designed to provide instruction and practice across as many—or as few—subject areas as is appropriate to help you achieve your goal. Read on to find out how to get the most out of this book based on your answers to the questions above.

## Your Learning Plan

- Begin with subjects for which you selected choice (C). The reference guide on page 9 indicates which chapters and sections you should review. Each subject has at least one short quiz; do not move on to a new subject until you have mastered these quizzes.

- Next, prioritize subjects for which you selected choice (B), again using the reference guide on page 9. Each subject has at least one short quiz; do not move on to an additional subject until you have mastered these quizzes.

- Read Parts 5 through 7 of this book to ensure understanding of the advice covered there.

- Take the quizzes in Part 8. If a quiz doesn't go well, determine what subjects need further review, and go back to the relevant chapter or chapters. Then re-take the quiz.

## Make a Game Plan

Set yourself up for success by making sure you know what you are doing and when!

Of the subjects listed in the reference guide below, circle Yes or No to indicate which subjects you will study. Use your answers to the questions above to decide.

# Reference Guide

| Subject | Chapter (Section) | I Will Work On This Subject | |
|---|---|---|---|
| *Parts of Speech* | 1 | Yes | No |
| *Elements of Sentences* | 2 | Yes | No |
| *Subject-Verb Agreement* | 3, A | Yes | No |
| *Pronoun-Noun Agreement* | 1, E | Yes | No |
| *Parallel Construction* | 3, B | Yes | No |
| *Misplaced Modifiers* | 3, C | Yes | No |
| *Faulty Comparisons* | 3, D | Yes | No |
| *Idioms* | 3, E | Yes | No |
| *Diction* | 3, F | Yes | No |
| *Redundancy* | 3, G | Yes | No |
| *Commas* | 4, B | Yes | No |
| *Periods versus Semicolons* | 4, A, E | Yes | No |
| *Colons* | 4, F | Yes | No |
| *Dashes* | 4, H | Yes | No |
| *Apostrophes* | 4, I | Yes | No |
| *Voice and Mood, Parentheses, Hyphens, Question Marks, Quotation Marks* | 3, H; 4, G, J, C, K, H | Yes | No |

I will devote ___ minutes on each of the following days to improving my grammar:

__ Monday   __ Tuesday   __ Wednesday   __ Thursday
__ Friday   __ Saturday   __ Sunday

# FAQ

Q: If a subject is not tagged to the SAT, ACT, or GMAT, does that mean the subject won't be tested?

A: Not necessarily. If we have tagged a grammar subject to a test, that subject is tested frequently on the test, such that you cannot avoid mastering the subject if you hope to achieve a high score. If your goal is to achieve a perfect score, however, you should master all subjects in this book.

Q: Aren't some rules of grammar and punctuation in dispute, such as whether a comma is needed before the word *and* in a list?

A: That is true. Where there is a lack of consensus, the rules in this book are taught consistently with the way the rules are tested on the SAT, ACT, and GMAT. Outside of standardized testing, you may consult the style guide of your choice or follow the style guide used by your school or workplace.

Q: You just mentioned style guides. I am hooked on grammar and usage and want to learn more. What should I read?

A: There are many classic works on grammar and usage. We recommend *The Chicago Manual of Style, Follett's Modern American Usage*, and *The Elements of Style* by Stunk and White. (Yes, we did include the comma before the word *and*!)

Q: I have completed this book, but there are still some topics that give me trouble. What help is available?

A: The Princeton Review offers academic tutoring, including for grammar, and also offers courses and tutoring for SAT, ACT, and GMAT. For more information, visit PrincetonReview.com or call 1-800-2REVIEW.

# Answers To Flawed Sentences

*Let's eat grandpa!*

Means: It's time to eat our grandpa. (Mmmmmm...grandpa.)

Corrected: Let's eat, grandpa!

*Toilet only for disabled elderly pregnant children.*

Means: The toilet can be used for those unique people who are both old and young and both pregnant and disabled.

Corrected: Toilet is for use by only those who are disabled, elderly, pregnant, or children.

*The Hunger Games star Josh Hutcherson has a new home as well as a new nose which used to be owned by the late Heath Ledger.*

Means: Josh Hutcherson bought Heath Ledger's nose. (Perhaps he bought it at an auction?)

Corrected: *The Hunger Games* star Josh Hutcherson has a new nose, as well as a new home, which used to be owned by the late Heath Ledger.

*Employees must wash all their hands prior to returning to work.*

Means: It is not enough for an employee to wash one or even two hands; all hands must be washed. (How many hands do you have?)

Corrected: All employees must wash their hands prior to returning to work.

*Eaten for good health, people enjoy fresh fruit for its sweet taste.*

Means: People are eaten for good health and, by the way, also enjoy fresh fruit for its sweet taste. (Mmmmmm. People.)

Corrected option 1: Eaten for good health, fresh fruit is enjoyed by many people for its sweet taste.

Corrected option 2: While people eat fresh fruit for good health, they enjoy the fruit for its sweet taste.

*We invited the strippers, Katy Perry and Jay-Z.*

Means: We invited the strippers, namely Katy Perry and Jay-Z. (That must have been quite the strip show!)

Corrected: We invited the strippers, Katy Perry, and Jay-Z.

# Final Thoughts

By using this book, you have shown yourself to be someone who identifies goals and sets out to achieve them. Because you will increase your knowledge of grammar, you will become a more effective communicator, both in writing and in speech. Sticking to a schedule and seeking out help when you need it will only add to your potential to achieve. The old saying "Knowledge is power" is especially true when it comes to understanding the rules of language; you're well on your way to owning English; what comes after that is up to you. And most importantly, enjoy the journey, which starts *now*!

# PART 1

# The Names of Things

"Parts of speech" is not exactly the kind of subject that usually comes up at parties—or at work either, for that matter. But even though you may not be aware of it, every time you speak or write you are nimbly (or not so nimbly) working with parts of speech, arranging your sentences according to parts of speech, and possibly even making jokes that hinge on parts of speech. What this chapter sets out to do is to broaden our already intuitive knowledge of parts of speech—to make the subject a little clearer and more useful to you.

Determining parts of speech is nothing more than determining the function a particular word has in a sentence. Different words, or groups of words, have different functions, and you will be able to avoid making errors—and put together a handsome sentence— if you are a whiz at determining parts of speech. Think of it like this: if you are going to build a table, you have to know what nails, screws, wood, nuts, and bolt look like, and also what their functions are. To understand parts of speech is to understand the materials of making sentences.

The most foolproof way to determine part of speech is to look up the word in a dictionary. The part of speech is listed, abbreviated and in italics, right after the pronunciation:

> perspicacious \ ,p ə r-spə -'ka -shəs\ *adj* [L
> *perspicac-, perspicax,* fr. *Perspicere*] (1640) :
> of acute mental vision or discernment: keen  *syn*
> see shrewd—perspicaciously *adv*—perspicaciousness
> *n*—perspicacity *n*

So what have we got here? *Perspicacious* means shrewd, smart, keen. It's an adjective, a word used to describe something or somebody. By making small changes to the ending, you can use the word as an adverb.

> Although he had poor grades, the student *perspicaciously* answered the questions in his oral exam.

Or as a noun.

> During his oral exam, the student demonstrated a great deal of *perspicacity*.

Again the difference between one part of speech and another is the role the word is performing. This chapter will show you the functions of the parts of speech, and from there we will move on to the big picture: the sentence.

# A. Nouns

Nouns are "people, place, and thing" words. It is easy to see that objects are nouns—things such as qualities and ideas can be nouns too—*love* is a noun, as is *egotism,* and *spoilage.* Nouns can be singular, when you are talking about one thing (*box*); and nouns can be plural, when you're talking about more than one thing (*boxes*).

Being able to spot nouns is important because the subject of a sentence is always a noun or a pronoun (we'll cover pronouns in a little while).

## Quick Quiz #1

*Circle the nouns and pronouns in the following paragraph:*

Zach Morris and Casey Jones are the hosts of a wonderful free show-case at Blast Masters Club featuring the best musicians based in the Kansas City area. Although they don't play any instruments, Zach and Casey are great at off-the-cuff banter. The musicians featured are the cream of the crop, and the headliner is a lady who uses the stage name Tooth Fairy. She is a hard rocker who hails from New York City and she never lets you forget that she's from the Big Apple. She has known Zach and Casey for over fifteen years and they typically all spend Sundays hanging out at a diner ten minutes away from the club.

# Rules for Nouns

1. If you aren't sure whether a word is a noun, put *a* or *the* in front of the word, and if that makes sense, the word is a noun. (a *mistake,* the *mood,* the *danger)*

2. Collective nouns are nouns that stand for an entire group, but are generally thought of as singular. *Family, committee,* and *furniture* are collective, because even though each noun contains more than one element, it is thought of as one group, and is therefore singular.

   The furniture *has* arrived. (collective noun, singular verb)

3. Nouns that have Latin endings are often mistaken for singular when they are really plural. Not every plural noun ends in -s. Watch out for the following words:

| singular | plural |
|---|---|
| alumna | alumnae (female) |
| alumnus | alumni (male) |
| bacterium | bacteria |
| criterion | criteria |
| datum | data |
| medium | media |
| memorandum | memoranda |

A singular subject takes a singular verb, and a plural subject takes a plural verb. Therefore:

The *alumnae* were whooping it up at their tenth reunion.
(plural *alumnae*, plural verb *were*)

During the Michael Jackson trial, the *media* were out of control.
(plural *media*, plural verb *were*)

4. Proper nouns are names of people, specific places, and particular groups and events. Proper nouns are always capitalized: LeBron James; Paris, Texas; Central Intelligence Agency; the War of the Roses.

5. Often, a word (or group of words) that looks like a verb acts as a noun. In other words, it is the subject of a verb. For example:

*Skiing* is Wanda's favorite sport.

*To know* me is to love me.

Wanda's favorite sport is a noun so even though *skiing* can be used as a verb (I *went skiing* today) in this case, *skiing* is acting as a noun, and is the subject of the verb *is*. This is called a gerund. *To know* is the infinitive form of the verb *know*. Here, *to know* is the subject of the verb *is*, so it, too, is acting as a noun. We'll cover this more in depth in Part 2.

---

## Quick Quiz #2

*In the following sentences, circle the nouns and label them singular, plural, or proper:*

1. The aliens sat on my Subaru and drank fruit juice.

2. The dance committee was considering all-black decorations for the prom.

3. My lunch is crawling with bacteria!

4. Swimming is very relaxing.

5. On Wednesday, Wanda went to Wichita to wait for Wilbur.

---

# B. Adjectives

Adjectives are descriptive words. *Gorgeous, hideous, smelly, baggy,* and *pathetic* are all adjectives. They describe or modify nouns.

Less obviously descriptive are adjectives that show which one or how many: *that* man, *his* dessert, *enough* meatloaf, *every* dog. See how the adjectives clarify which noun (or how many of each noun) is being talked about? (See Quick Quiz #3 below)

## Quick Quiz #3

*Circle the adjectives in the paragraphs below.*

The day Billy was born dark thunder clouds swept across the sky. His loving parents glanced out the hospital window and saw jagged lightning crash to the ground.

"Is this a bad omen?" Billy's balding mother asked.

"Don't be superstitious," Billy's balding father said, but secretly he wondered whether the scary weather would forebode trouble for young Billy. Billy's father had seen *Rosemary's Baby* earlier that week, and he peeked into the brand-new bassinet to see if Billy looked like a newborn baby or a newborn monster.

As Billy grew up his parents were relieved to see how normal he was. Billy talked back to his parents, destroyed the house, refused to eat green vegetables, and came home bloody from the playground just like any other kid.

Billy's parents were none too perceptive, and there were other, more subtle signs—signs that Billy was weirder than you average child— that they failed to see.

# Rules for Adjectives

1. An adjective like *ugly* can be relative; in other words, you aren't necessarily either ugly or not ugly—you can be ugly to degrees. To show this kind of comparison, there are three forms of adjectives:

   | positive | comparative | superlative |
   |----------|-------------|-------------|
   | ugly | uglier | ugliest |
   | great | greater | greatest |

   If you are comparing only one thing to another, from the comparative by adding -*er* to the adjective.

   My dog is *uglier* than your dog.

   If you are comparing more than two things, form the superlative by adding -*est* to the adjective.

   My dog is the *ugliest* dog on earth.

2. Some adjectives do not lend themselves to adding -*er* or -*est* to the stem. In these cases, use *more* as the comparative and *most* as the superlative. Your ear should be able to discern which form is appropriate; when in doubt, use *more* or *most*.

   Your dog is *more beautiful* than my dog.

   That is the *most unbelievable* thing I have ever heard.

3. Some adjectives are absolute—you either have the quality or you don't. So there is no comparative or superlative for adjectives such as *perfect, dead, square*, or *essential*.

   You can't be deader that someone else who is only dead. And you know from geometry that squares must have four equal sides and four right angles—so a shape either conforms to that definition or it doesn't. *Essential* means necessary; the quality isn't relative.

Keep in mind that when advertisers scream "This soap will make your whites whiter!" they may sell more detergent, but they are misusing an absolute adjective.

---

## Absolute adjectives:

| | | |
|---|---|---|
| absolute | basic | certain |
| complete | empty | entire |
| devoid | excellent | fatal |
| final | dead | perfect |
| square | essential | unique |
| full | harmless | immortal |
| meaningless | obvious | pure |
| superior | ultimate | universal |

---

You get the idea. If you're wondering about a word that's not on the list, think about its meaning. Does it seem to express an absolute quality?

4. Adjectives that describe how much or how many are often misused. If you are talking about something that you can count individually, use *fewer* or *many*. If you are talking about something that can't be counted individually—something that's more like a blob, or a quantity—use *less, a lot of, much.*

I ate *fewer* french fries than you did.

You ate *less* mashed potatoes than I did.

## Quick Quiz #4

### Identifying Adjectives

*Circle the appropriate adjective:*

1. Last night I ate (fewer, less) marshmallows than Wanda did.

2. She considered the marshmallow to be (a perfect, the most perfect) food.

3. In rating marshmallows and oysters, Wanda liked marshmallows (best, better).

4. "A marshmallow is (spongier than, the spongiest of) any other food," she said.

5. Although she ate (many, much) marshmallows, she ate (fewer, less) Jell-O.

**Adjective Trivia Question:** In some languages, French for example, adjectives of a certain type precede the noun, and others follow the noun. In English, adjectives almost always come before the noun: a *happy* fellow, *green* apples. Now for bonus points: name an English adjective that is placed after the noun it modifies. Check your answer at the bottom of this page by turning this book upside down.

*Adjective Trivia Answer:*
*galore, aplenty.*

# C. Verbs

Without a verb, you have no sentence. Verbs express either action (like *hit*, *sprint*, or *touch*) or state-of-being (like *am*, *seems*, *will be*). The first kind of verb is called an action verb; the second kind is called a linking verb. This distinction is not anything to worry about; we only mention it to show the various functions of different kinds of verbs.

Put another way, a verb tells what the subject is doing or what is being done to the subject, even if the subject is doing nothing more than just existing.

The rules for verbs chiefly concern two characteristics: tense, and agreement with the subject. Tense is discussed below; for agreement, see Part 3, Section A.

## Tense

The tense of a verb places the action at a particular time. The English language has twelve tenses altogether, so we are able to be quite precise in explaining when something happened. Although memorizing the names of the tenses is not terribly important, you do want to understand which moment in time each tense refers to. The six basic tenses are:

| | | | |
|---|---|---|---|
| *present*: | I eat | *present perfect*: | I have eaten |
| *past*: | I ate | *past perfect*: | I had eaten |
| *future*: | I will eat | *future perfect*: | I will have eaten |

Now let's take a look at what moment in time each tense indicates.

**Present:** The "now" tense. Use the present tense if

1. The action is happening right now: I *am* hungry (right now).

2. The action happens habitually: I *am* hungry every afternoon.

3. You are stating a fact: Elvis Costello *is* a great songwriter.

4. You want dramatic effect in fiction, or in expository writing: The phone *rings*. Fitzgerald *is* more interesting than Hemingway. (This use of the present is called the historical present.)

5. You are speaking about the future (this is more informal, and if this seems confusing, you can always safely use the tense to about the future): She *leaves* for Paris in the morning. (Or: She *will leave* for Paris in the morning.)

**Present Perfect:** Use the present perfect if

1. The action started in the past and continues into the present moment: I *have eaten* sixteen cookies so far this week.

2. The action was finished at some earlier time but affects the present: I *have eaten* all of the pie, so there isn't any left for you.

**Past:** The "before" tense. Use the past tense if

1. The action happened in the past and does not continue to happen: I *ate* it.

**Past Perfect:** The "even before before" tense. Use the past perfect if

1. You are discussing an action already in the past, and you need to make clear that another action happened even earlier. Think of past perfect as the double past tense: Before I *ate* your dessert, I *had eaten* 87 doughnuts. (*Ate* is past tense, *had eaten* is past perfect.)

2. You have an "if" clause followed by the conditional (would) and the present perfect: *If* I *had thought* about it first, I *would not have eaten* all those doughnuts.

**Future:** The *Star Trek* tense. All statements using future tense have not yet happened—they are in the future. (This is all pretty logical, isn't it?) Use the future tense if

1. You are talking about something that will happen in the future: Tomorrow I *will go* on a diet.

**Future Perfect:** This tense combines future and past—and it doesn't come up very often. Use future perfect if

1. An action is finished before a specified time in the future: By next week I *will have lost* ten pounds.

In addition to these six tenses are the continuous (or progressive) forms of all six. As with the whole subject of tenses, the names of the tenses are not important—what is important is being able to use the right tense in the right situation. The continuous tenses use the -*ing* verb, or present participle: I *am eating*, I *was eating*, I *will be eating*. Use the continuous form if

1. You want to show continuous action: I *will be dieting* for eternity.

---

**Quick Quiz #5**

**Are You Tense?**

*Write the correct verb form in the blanks below. The verb to use is given in the infinitive form at the end of the sentence.*

1. Today Lulu _____ for Alfred to call her. (to wait)

2. Yesterday Lulu _____ at Alfred because he _____ her birthday. (to scream, to forget)

3. Tomorrow, if he is smart, Alfred _____ her bunches of flowers. (to give)

4. If he _____, he would not be in so much trouble. ( to remember)

5. By next week Alfred and Lulu _____ fun again. (to have)

---

# More on Verbs

If you've ever studied a foreign language, you know about conjugating verbs. For most verbs, your ear will match the correct verb to your subject—it doesn't take any special thought to say *I go* instead of *I goes*. First, some terms.

**Person:** This applies only when you have an actual person as the subject of the verb.

|  | **Singular** | **Plural** |
|---|---|---|
| First person | I | we |
| Second person | you | you |
| Third person | he/she | they |

**Number:** Number is simply the differences between singular and plural.

**Present Participle:** The *-ing* verb form. This form of the verb goes with *is* or *are* to form the continuous tenses: is *walking*, are *swearing*, is *loving*.

**Past Participle:** The form of the verb that goes with *have* to form the present perfect: have *walked*, have *sworn*, have *loved*.

**Infinitive:** The infinitive is the "to" form of the verb, as in *to go, to do, to see*. For rules on infinitives, see Part 2, Section D.

Deciding on the right verb form presents no problem if the verb is regular. A regular verb is conjugated like any other regular verb.

I move, I moved, I am moving, I have moved

I walk, I walked, I am walking, I have walked

The trouble arises when the verb is irregular, and doesn't fit into the pattern of an added *-ed* to make the past tense and past participle: I walk*ed*, I have walk*ed*. Many irregular verbs—like the verb *to be*—are used so frequently that their irregularity is not a problem, because you know the principal parts by heart, even if you'd never heard of the term *principal parts* before opening this book.

Here's a list of headache-causing irregular verbs as well as some regular verbs that are often misused.

# Principal Parts

| present | past | past participle |
| --- | --- | --- |
| bear | bore | borne |
| blow | blew | blown |
| bring | brought | brought (*not brang*) |
| creep | crept | crept |
| dive | dived | dived (*dove* only informally; not *diven*) |
| drag | dragged | dragged |
| draw | drew | drawn |
| drink | drank | drunk |
| freeze | froze | frozen |
| get | got | got, gotten |
| grow | grew | grown |
| hang | hung | hung (as in *I hung a picture on the wall*) |
| hang | hanged | hanged (as in *The man was hanged at sunrise*) |

| | | |
|---|---|---|
| lay | laid | laid |
| | | (as in *I laid the book on the bed*) |
| lend | lent | lent |
| lie | lay | lain |
| | | (as in *I have lain in bed all day*) |
| ring | rant | rung |
| shake | shook | shaken |
| shrink | shrank, shrunk | shrunk, shrunken |
| sink | sank | sunk |
| | | (not *sinked*) |
| slay | slew | slain |
| spring | sprang, sprung | sprung |
| swear | swore | sworn |
| swim | swam | swum |
| tear | tore | torn |
| weep | wept | wept |
| wring | wrung | wrung |

# D. Adverbs

Adverbs modify verbs (run *quickly*), adjectives (*often* happy), or other adverbs (*too* quickly). Adverbs frequently end in *-ly*, but the *-ly* isn't a requirement. A test for determining adverbs is to think about function: adverbs tend to tell where, when, or how.

> *very* ugly; *most* unpleasant; *never* sleepy; *slightly*
>
> askew; come *soon*; groan *loudly*

**Possible Confusion:** Adjectives also modify, so it is easy to confuse them with adverbs. And even more confusingly, some words sometimes act as adjectives, and sometimes act as adverbs, depending on the sentence and the circumstance. Ask yourself which word is being described: adjectives always modify nouns or pronouns, and adverbs never do.

Wanda was a *little* sleepy.

(adverb *little* modifying adjective *sleepy*)

Wanda took a *little* nap.

(adjective *little* modifying noun *nap*)

# Rules for Adverbs

1. Adverbs follow the same form as adjectives when they are used to make comparisons.

| positive | comparative | superlative |
|----------|-------------|-------------|
| soon | sooner | soonest |
| little | less | least |
| drunkenly | more drunkenly | most drunkenly |

2. In placing adverbs, follow a simple rule: put the adverb as close as possible to the word being modified. Otherwise you may be giving your sentence a meaning other than the one you intend.

My headache was *only* temporary.

*Only* my headache was temporary.

How does the meaning of the sentence change when the adverb is moved?

## Quick Quiz #7

### Billy Wifflamoo, the Early Years

*Circle five adverbs in the follwing passage.*

Billy's third grade teacher was a hearty woman named Mrs. Dingdong. Mrs. Dingdong spoke loudly, and her booming voice could often be heard by students in surrounding buildings. Her students would later confess that they heard Mrs. Dingdong's booming voice in their dreams for the rest of their lives.

"Billy!" Mrs. Dingdong boomed fondly. "You are almost the messiest boy ever born! Quickly put your paste and your scissors in your locker and stand quietly in line!"

Billy shook with fear when Mrs. Dingdong boomed at him. He understood well enough that she was only trying to educate him, but his ears were extremely sensitive and the reverberations of her voice lasted over the weekend.

---

***Adverb Trivia Question:*** An awful lot of adverbs end in *-ly.* Can you name some adjectives that end in *-ly?* How about a noun ending in *-ly?* Check the bottom of the page for answers.

*Adverb Trivia Answers:*
Adjectives: *oily, hilly, friendly.*
Noun: *Contumely, which means insult.*

# E. Pronouns

Pronouns are a subgroup of nouns; they act as stand-ins for nouns. There are eight categories of pronouns, but a few simple rules govern their use. First, let's go over some terms.

**Case** refers to the function of the pronoun in the sentence. The three cases are nominative, objective, and possessive. Think of these as subject pronouns, object pronouns, and ownership pronouns.

**Number** makes a pronoun either singular or plural.

**Gender** specifies whether the person a pronoun refers to is a man or a woman.

An **antecedent** is the noun (usually appearing earlier in the sentence or paragraph than the pronoun) that the pronoun stands in for in the sentence.

## Personal Pronouns

**Subject pronouns** (nominative case): *I, you, he, she, it, we,* and *they.* All of these will be the subject of a verb.

> *It* is alive! (*It* is the subject of *is*)

> Wanda knew exactly what *she* should do. (*she* is the subject of *should do*)

**Object pronouns** (objective case): *me, you, him, her it, us, them.* These are always the object of the verb, preposition, or infinitive— never the subject. In other words, object pronouns are having something done to them, rather than doing the action themselves.

Wanda showered *him* with insults. (the *him* isn't doing anything—
he's receiving the insults, not showering them)

He wanted *her* to go to a movie with *him*. (*He* is the subject of
*wanted*; *her* is the object of *wanted*; *him* is the object of the
preposition *with*)

**Ownership pronouns** (possessive case): *mine, yours, his, hers, its,
ours, theirs.* They are used to show ownership, answering the question "Whose?"

The dog was *hers*. (Whose dog? *Her* dog)

## Rules for Personal Pronouns

1.  Subject pronouns follow the verb *to be.*

It is *I*! (*I* follows *is*)

It was *they* who ate all the cookies. (*they* follows *was*)

Casually talking to each other we would more naturally say *It's
me,* or *It was them*—so this rule applies mostly to formal writing.
Again, base your choice on the situation.

2. If you're having trouble deciding whether to use a subject or object pronoun, ignore parts of the sentence that get in the way.

Tell the secret to Bob and (I, me).

Read as: Tell the secret to (I, me).

Now your ear should help you out: Tell the secret *to me*. Therefore: Tell the secret *to Bob and me*. The main difficulty arises when another person gets between the preposition and the pronoun—so get the other person out of the way, and you will choose correctly.

3. Case is tricky when it comes to infinitives. If the infinitive *to be* has no subject, use a subject pronoun that agrees with the subject of the sentence.

Donna seems to be *she* who is making the anonymous calls.

For other infinitives, or if the infinitive *to be* has a subject, use an object pronoun.

Her boss considered the best candidate to be *her*.

Does this seem to be a difficult, awkward rule? Do the example sentences above seem forced—exactly the kind of thing that makes learning about grammar a big bore? Here's where some common sense and creativity come in: when you are working with a sentence that is caught in a web of rules—and if following those rules leaves you with a sentence that sounds particularly awkward—just do what writers spend most of their time doing: Rewrite! Like this:

It seems to be Donna who is making the anonymous calls.

Her boss considered her to be the best candidate.

Or: Her boss considered her the best candidate.

---

## The Golden Rule: Avoid Trouble

Knotty rules can almost always be avoided by writing more simply and more clearly. Remember, the point of understanding the rules of grammar is to be able to express your thoughts more precisely, not to write sentences that call attention to your knowledge of grammar. Editing is like housecleaning—if you're doing it well, no one should notice the work that's gone into it. It's only when the work hasn't been done that you look sloppy.

---

4. When making a comparison (using *as* or *than*) choose the case of pronoun that would finish the clause.

Max wanted to stay out later than *she*. (than she did)

Occasionally, misapplying this rule can garble your meaning.

Max loved ice cream more than *her*.

(he loved ice cream more than he loved her)

Max loved ice cream more than *she*.

(he loved ice cream more than she loved ice cream)

So which is it? Again, you can avoid the ambiguity problem by writing.

Max loved ice cream more than Wanda did.

Or: Max loved ice cream more than he loved Wanda.

Now there isn't any doubt about the meaning. (For Wanda's sake, let's hope for the first version.) We'll talk more about this in Part 3, Section E.

# Mirror Pronouns

Mirror pronouns, also called reflexive pronouns, reflect the action of the verb back at the subject. The mirror pronouns are *myself, yourself, himself, herself, ourselves, yourselves, themselves, itself.*

## Rules for Using Mirror Pronouns

1. Use the appropriate mirror pronoun to match the subject.

*She* hit *herself* with the hammer.

*They* took *themselves* to lunch.

2. You may also use mirror pronouns for emphasis, but don't get carried away.

*I myself* was left bleeding on the sidewalk.

The director *herself* took a cut in salary.

Bob and *I* ate some tacos.

**Not:** Bob and *myself* ate some tacos.

The waiter brought the tacos to Bob and *me*.

**Not:** The waiter brought the tacos to Bob and *myself*.

# Relative Pronouns

These pronouns link a subordinate, or relative, clause to the main clause of the sentence. They also act as stand-ins for nouns, just as all pronouns do. The definite relative pronouns are *which, that,* and *who* (or *whom,* if you're using the objective form of *who.*) The indefinite relative pronouns are *what, which, who, whatever, whom,* and *whomever.* The difference between definite and indefinite relative pronouns is that indefinite pronouns aren't clearly standing in for a noun already in the sentence—they have no antecedent. This is not a distinction you need to lose sleep over.

Wanda went to Mabel, *who* had given her good advice in the post.

The main clause of the sentence is *Wanda went to see Mabel. Who had given her good advice in the past* is a relative clause—it can't stand by itself as a sentence—modifying Mabel. The relative pronoun *who* links this clause to the main part of the sentence. We'll talk more about relative clauses in Part 2, Section E.

## Rules for Relative Pronouns

1. Use *who* if the pronoun is the subject of a verb. Use *whom* if the pronoun is the object of a verb, preposition, or infinitive.

   > Mabel wondered *who* was ringing her doorbell.

   > (*who* is the subject of *was ringing*)

   > Mabel was not sure whom she could trust with her secret.

   > (*Mabel* is the subject of *trust*; *whom* is the object of *trust*.)

   > Wanda asked Mabel *who* had given her the documents.

   > Mabel told her it was a man with *whom* she had worked last year.

   Deciding between *who* and *whom* is not so difficult—simply decide whether an object pronoun such as *him* or *me* would be appropriate, and if it is, use *whom*. Another way to decide is to see if the pronoun is doing an action. Is it the subject of a verb? Use *who*. If the sentence begins with the pronoun, you are safe using *who*.

   > "Who did you tell?" asked Wanda.

   > **Or:** "Whom did you tell?" asked Wanda.

   Either of these is acceptable, although clearly the second version is more formal.

2. *Who* and *whom* are used to refer only to people.

3. *That* can refer to people, animals, and things.

4. *Which* cannot refer to people.

5. *That* and *which* are often misused. If your relative clause is a defining clause (also called a restrictive clause) *that* is the better choice. A defining clause limits the group being defined; we are meant to think only of part of the group, instead of the whole. The following sentences are a couple of examples:

> Dogs *that* have three legs can learn to hop quickly.

> Dogs, *which* can be trained to do nearly anything, love to work and to play.

In the first sentence we are talking about a limited group of dogs—three-legged dogs, not all the dogs in the world. That makes *that have three legs* a defining clause, and to introduce a defining clause, use *that.* In the second sentence *which can be trained to do almost anything* is talking about all dogs, not a specific group. The clause does not serve to define which dogs we mean. So use *which.*

Commas are critical here. A clause set off by commas is not crucial to the sentence—and if the clause isn't necessary, it isn't a defining clause, and so takes which. To sum up: if the clause is set off by commas, use *which.* If the clause has no commas, use that.

# Question Pronouns

Question pronouns (also called interrogative pronouns) are used, unsurprisingly, to ask questions. The question pronouns are *which, who, whom,* and *what.*

*Which* dog has three legs?

*Who* ate my cake?

*What* were you thinking?

# Pointing Pronouns

Pointing pronouns (also called demonstrative pronouns) are used to indicate which thing you are talking about. The pointing pronouns are *that, these, this, those.*

### Rules for Pointing Pronouns

1. A pointing pronoun, like any pronoun, has to stand in for a noun, or else it is an adjective.

> Get a load of *this*! (pointing pronoun, no antecedent)

> *This* teacher is incredibly boring. (adjective, modifying *teacher*)

> I want to eat all of *these*. (*these* standing in for Fritos, burritos, or whatever the speaker in pointing to)

> I want to eat all of *these* burritos. (*these* modifying *burritos*)

2. As with all pronouns, you should make sure your audience understands what you pronoun stands for. A pointing pronoun doesn't require an antecedent in the sentence, but the antecedent should still be clear. For instance, in the example above *Get a load of this!* The audience presumably knows what *this* the speaker or writer is talking about. See Last Words on Pronoun Agreement, Part 3, Section A.

# Indefinite Pronouns

Indefinite pronouns are vague; they don't stand in for specific nouns.

### Indefinite pronouns

| | | | |
|---|---|---|---|
| all | any | anybody | anything |
| both | each | either | enough |
| everybody | everything | few | less |
| many | more | much | neither |
| none | nothing | one | plenty |
| several | some | someone | |

The rules for indefinite pronouns mostly concern gender and number, so it might be helpful to review these terms in Part 3

## Rules for Indefinite Pronouns

1. *Each, every, anybody, anything, somebody,* and *something* are always singular, so use a singular verb and a singular personal pronoun to match.

> *Each* of the boys wants a pizza for himself.
> (*each* takes the singular verb *wants* and the singular personal pronoun *himself*)

> Is *anybody* going to eat the last pepperoni?
> (*anybody* takes the singular verb *is*)

**Possible Confusion:** How do you know if a verb is singular or plural? As you can see in the example above, *each wants*, a singular verb often ends in *-s*. But there are many exceptions. The easy way to find a singular verb form is to match the verb with *he* or *she*, which is singular. Your ear will match it correctly. Use *they* if you are looking for the plural form of the verb. *She wants, they want.* See Part 3 Section A.

2. *Both, several, few, many,* and *plenty* always refer to more than one thing; therefore, they are always plural. Match them with plural verbs and plural personal pronouns (they, them, their).

> *Both* of the pizzas were delivered cold.
> (*both* takes the plural verb *were*)

> *Many* of the boys eat their cookies before eating their salads.
> (*Many* takes the plural verb *eat* and the plural personal pronoun *their*)

3. *All, most,* and *some* can be singular or plural. If you are talking about things that can be counted individually, like coins or socket wrenches, treat the pronoun as plural.

*Most* of the greedy felons *are* going to jail.
(the felons are individuals, so *most* takes the plural verb *are*)

*Some* of the differences between them *are* apparent.
(the differences are specific, individual, countable things, so *some* takes the plural verb *are*)

If you are talking about things that aren't individually countable—quantities you can pour, like water or sand or beer, or things that you can't divide into discrete parts, like love or anger—treat the pronoun as singular.

*Most* of the attention *is* on the trader guilty of securities fraud.

*Some* of the beer *is* spilling on the rug.

4. *None* is usually treated as plural, unless you are using it in the sense of *not one single thing,* or *no one person.*

*None* of the politicians *is* solely responsible for the miserable state of the economy. (*none* meaning *no one person*)

*None* were happy. (*none* meant as a plural group of individuals)

# F. Prepositions

Prepositions express relationships between other words, usually nouns, including relationships of time or space. *In, of, to,* and *with* are all prepositions. A helpful trick to determine whether a word is a preposition is to place it before "the fence."

*Beyond* the fence, *past* the fence, *over* the fence, *under* the fence, *of* the fence, *across* the fence—all of these constructions make some kind of sense, so all the italicized words are prepositions, just doing their job: defining relationships. "The fence" is the object of the preposition.

# Rules for Prepositions

1. Use *between* when you're talking about two things or groups; use *among* for more than two things.

> Wanda couldn't decide *between* the motorcycle and the Jet Ski.

> The lottery prize was divided *among* the three winners.

> Ralph was choosing *between* the Democratic and Libertarian parties.

**Possible Confusion:** Note that even though the Democratic and Libertarian parties are made up of millions of people, *between* is still appropriate, because Ralph is considering only two choices—Democratic and Libertarian. Don't worry about the total number of elements, just figure out how many choices there are.

**Prepositions:**

| | | | | |
|---|---|---|---|---|
| across | after | at | as | before |
| between | by | for | from | in |
| like | of | on | over | through |
| to | under | until | up | with |

2. A commonly heard grammatical law is: Never end a sentence with a preposition. Well, may, maybe not. If you want to sound formal—for a paper at school, or a memo at work—put the preposition in the middle of the sentence and add a word such as *which* or *whom*.

> I picked up a rock *with which* to hit him.

Or more informally:

> I picked up a rock to hit him *with*.

As above, the content of the sentence may indicate which choice is better. If putting the preposition in the middle of the sentence sounds unpleasantly awkward, just leave it at the end.

3. Many idioms require you to use a particular preposition with a particular word. For example, we say: *Listen to* Destiny's Child, not *Listen at* Destiny's Child. She is *involved in* her work, not She is *involved by* her work. For a thorough look at the idiomatic usage of prepositions, see Part 3, Section E.

# G. Conjunctions

Conjunctions connect words or parts of sentences—*conjoin* means to join together. We'll cover parts of sentences (phrases and clauses) in Part 2; you may want to flip back to this section after you understand how to recognize phrases and clauses. There are three categories of conjunctions.

# Coordinating Conjunctions

Also known as matchmaking conjunctions, these words connect equal parts of sentences. In other words, they connect words to words, phrases to phrases, and clauses to clauses.

> Wanda *and* Max were late to the party.
> (noun to noun)
> Wanda spent the day playing the sax *or* walking the dog.
> (phrase to phrase)
> Max hated his job, *but* he couldn't afford to quit.
> (clause to clause)

List of matchmaking conjunctions: *and, or, but, for, nor, so, yet.*

# Correlative Conjunctions

Also known as seesaw conjunctions, these words also connect equal parts together (they are really a subcategory of matchmaking conjunctions). The difference is that seesaw conjunctions are really two conjunctions in one.

> *Either* Wanda *or* Max would get promoted.

> Wanda wanted *not only* fame and riches *but also* love.

List of seesaw conjunctions: *both-and, either-or, neither-nor, not only-but also.*

# Subordinating Conjunctions

Also known as linking conjunctions, these words connect dependent, or subordinate, clauses with the independent, or main, clause. The subordinate clauses act as nouns or as adverbs.

Max quit his job *because* he was bored.

He later realized he should have waited *until* he had a new job.

Now he had to decide *what to do next*.

*Because he was bored* answers the question *Why did Max quit?* so the clause is functioning as an adverb. *Until he had a new job* answers the question *How long should Max have waited?* so it, too, is an adverb clause. *What to do next* answers the question *What did Max have to decide?* so it is a noun clause. These clauses aren't sentences themselves—they can't stand alone. They need to be connected to the main clauses *Max quit his job* and *He later realized he should have waited.* The linking conjunction acts as the link, connecting the subordinate clause to the main clause.

## Identifying Conjunctions

*In each of the following sentences, underline the matchmaking or seesaw conjunction and circle the words, phrases, or clauses connected by the conjunction.*

1. Reginald loved bathing and shaving.

2. He was obsessed with cleanliness, but his closet was a mess.

3. Reginald not only took four showers every day but also washed his clothes twice.

4. He was either afraid of germs or afraid of looking unkempt.

5. Reginald spent yesterday and today pruning his face of every stray hair.

## Linking conjunctions:

| after | although | as | as if |
|---|---|---|---|
| as long as | because | before | but that |
| even if | except that | ever since | if |
| if only | in case | just as | since |
| unless | until | when | whenever |
| where | wherever | while | |

**More on Identifying Conjunctions**

*In each of the following sentences, underline the linking conjunction and place brackets around the subordinate clause.*

1. Reginald was late to work because he washed his hair 16 times.

2. Since his boss was also obsessed with cleanliness, Reginald was not reprimanded for being late.

3. Reginald will not have much of a social life as long as he considers everyone too cavalier regarding hygiene.

4. Until he cleans that messy closet, he will not sleep well at night.

5. Reginald is obsessed with filth because he does not want to think about anything else.

# H. Interjections

*Wow! Heavens above!* Interjections are the most fun part of speech! Curses are in this category: *Damn! Hey!* Are interjections that function as filler, or as a kind of introductory word, often to show emphasis. And the good news is: no rules apply, except possibly good taste. *Cool!*

# I. Articles

Articles introduce nouns: *this* is the definite article, *a* and *an* are indefinite articles. Try using them in a sentence to understand the distinction between definite and indefinite.

A mouse could be any mouse, anywhere.

The mouse specifies definitely—the mouse in my room, for example.

Articles have a simple function—to point out, or introduce, a noun. Think of them as adjectives, since they are really describing the nouns they introduce.

# Summary

- **The term "parts of speech":** refers to the way a word is used in a sentence; the part of speech of a particular word can be found by looking up the word in the dictionary.

- **Nouns:** are people, place, or thing words. Ideas and qualities are also nouns. Only nouns, or words or phrases that act as nouns, can be the subject of a sentence. (ex: *rat, happiness, democracy*)

- **Adjectives:** describe or modify nouns. They describe by saying which one, how many, how much, or what kind of noun you mean. (ex: *chartreuse, mealy, tremendous*)

- **Verbs:** tell what the noun is doing. They express either action or a state of being. Every sentence must have a verb. (ex: *is, was cleaning, had buried.*)

- **Tense:** is the form of the verb that places the action in time. Past tense puts the action in the past; present tense puts the action at the current time. There are six basic tense, plus the continuous, or *-ing* forms, of all six.

- **Adverbs:** modify verbs, adjectives, or other adverbs. They describe by saying when, in what manner, where, how, or how much. An adverb never modifies a noun. (ex: *haughtily, almost, feverishly*)

- **Pronouns:** act as stand-ins for nouns. (ex: *me, whom, everyone*)

- **Prepositions:** link nouns to other words in a sentence, usually describing a relationship of time or space. (ex: *of, to, with*)

- **Conjunctions:** link words or parts of sentences. (ex: *and, yet, either/or*)

- **Interjections:** provide emphasis and filler; there are no rules to worry about. (ex: *Wow! Ugh! Aiyiyi!*)

**Parts of Speech**

Julie Andrews went for raindrops on roses and whiskers on kittens—what are a few of your favorite things? List your five favorite nouns.

1.

2.

3.

4.

5.

Now think of an adjective to describe each of your favorite nouns.

1.

2.

3.

4.

5.

What would be the correct pronoun for each of your nouns?

1.

2.

3.

4.

5.

With your adjective-noun pairs, make prepositional phrases.

1.

2.

3.

4.

5.

List your five favorite verbs.

1.

2.

3.

4.

5.

Now think of an adverb to modify each verb.

1.

2.

3.

4.

5.

# Batting Practice, Part 1

The following drills test nearly everything we've discussed in Part 1.

## Drill 1

*Pick the best answer. If you don't find an error, pick choice A.*

1. Gomez thought Pinky's hairstyle <u>was the most unique, but whom had designed</u> her hideous dress?

   A) was the most unique, but whom had designed

   B) was the most unique, but who designed

   C) to be the most unique, but whom had designed

   D) was unique, but who had been designing

   E) was unique, but who had designed


2. The dresses <u>which hung on the rack were made for Pinky and I</u>.

   A) which hung on the rack were made for Pinky and I

   B) which hung on the rack were made for Pinky and me

   C) that were hanging on the rack having been made for Pinky and I

   D) that hung on the rack were made for Pinky and me

   E) hanged on the rack and they were made for me and Pink

3. <u>The one criteria you must meet to dress well is knowing what cut is right for one's body</u>.

    A) The one criteria you must meet to dress well is knowing what cut is right for one's body.

    B) To dress well, the one criteria you must meet is to know what cut is right for your body.

    C) In dressing well, the one criterion you must meet is knowing what cut is right for one's body.

    D) To dress well, the one criterion you must meet is to know what cut is right for your body.

    E) The one criterion you must meet, for dressing well, is knowing what cut is right for your body.

4. In 1978, a peak of nonfashion, <u>great amounts of people wear</u> polyester jackets.

    A) great amounts of people wear

    B) great amounts of people were wearing

    C) great numbers of people wore

    D) a great amount of people wore

    E) large numbers of people are wearing

5. Now that it is 2001, pumps and tight jeans <u>will be back on the runway, but her and me have less of these</u> retro items in our closets.

A) will be back on the runway, but her and me have less of these

B) will be back on the runway, but she and me will have fewer of these

C) are back on the runway, but she and I have fewer of these

D) are being back on the runway, but she and I have less of these

E) are back on the runway, but her and I have fewer of these

# Drill 2

*Circle the error. If you find no error, circle choice E.*

1. The novelist, the <u>most talented</u> of the two writers <u>who</u> came over
   A       B

   for dinner, <u>slipped</u> on a tennis ball <u>that was lying</u> on the rug in
   C      D

   the hallway. ___
   E

2. The screenwriter was <u>deliriously happy</u> <u>to see</u> that Pinky and Bob
   A   B

   had <u>began</u> to cook the cabbage <u>and grill</u> the steaks. ____
   C      D    E

3. <u>That the writers</u> had not been able to afford <u>anything but</u> beans and
   A       B

   rice was <u>evident in their delight</u> at sitting down to the feast, and in
   C

   the dangerous speed <u>with which</u> they inhaled their food. ____
   D       E

4. The <u>argument among</u> the two writers <u>was</u> not a scholarly
   A       B

   dispute; they were simply <u>trying to divide</u> the last piece of cake
   C

   <u>between them.</u> ____
   D  E

5. The novelist, <u>who modeled himself</u> after Hemingway, wrestled
   A

   the cake away from the screenwriter, <u>who was known for</u> <u>constant</u>
   B     C

   changing artistic direction; sometimes he <u>wrote like</u> Godard, and
   D

   sometimes like Spielberg. ____
   E

# Drill 3

Identify the part of speech of every word in the following sentences.

1. I am shivering from the cold.

2. I made delicious pot roast and beans and rice for dinner.

3. There is nothing better than pot roast, in my opinion.

4. Yikes! I somehow left my hat in the oven!

5. Actually we would rather order Chinese food and watch TV, because we can eat these fortune cookies and stand on our heads until we are ready for bed.

# Party On with Parts of Speech

Now for some fun. You need a friend for this game. The reader takes the following story, without letting the other person see any part of it (including the title) and asks the other person to name the parts of speech listed under the blanks. The reader writes the answers in the blanks; when all the blanks are filled, the reader reads the story aloud. Hilarity ensues.

Abbreviations:  ADJ: adjective
ADV: adverb
PRO: pronoun
SUB. PRO: subject pronoun
COLL. NOUN: collective noun
REFL. PRO: reflexive pronoun (mirror pronoun)
SUPER. ADJ: superlative adjective
COMP. ADJ: comparative adjective
SEESAW CONJ: seesaw conjunction
(coordinating conjunction)
GER: gerund
OWN. PRO: ownership pronoun
PL. NOUN: plural noun
INDEF. PRO: indefinite pronoun

## The Perfect Date

To get ready, I fixed my _____ and put on my _____. I
                        NOUN                      NOUN

wanted to look _____, because I was so _____ and _____.
                ADJ                    ADJ    ADJ

_____ took me to see a _____ and then we went to
SUB. PRO                   NOUN

a _____ and ate _____ and drank _____. Afterward, while
  NOUN         NOUN         NOUN

_____ down the street, _____held my _____ then kissed
GER              SUB. PRO      NOUN

my _____. _____ looked _____ in the moonlight.
   NOUN   SUB. PRO      ADJ

_____ thoughts were _____ and I was _____
OWN PRO              PL. NOUN          ADJ

_____ _____. I felt _____. I wished the night would never
ADJ   ADJ        ADJ

_____. The next morning I was _____. My date had been
VERB                    ADJ

_____ _____.
ADV   ADJ

## How to Choose a College

Several _____ questions must be
             ADJ
answered before you start the application process.

1. What is the ratio of _____ to _____?
              PL. NOUN   PL. NOUN

2. How big is the school? _____ students or _____
                      INDEF. PRO            INDEF. PRO
  students?

3. Can you get academic credit for _____, _____, or _____?
                            GER   GER     GER

4. Is the climate _____ or _____?
              ADJ    ADJ

5. Do the students like to _____, or would they rather _____?
                  VERB                 VERB

6. What is the school's strongest department? _____, or
                                     GER
  _____?
  GER

7. Will you be required to take a foreign _____? For _____
                               NOUN     NUMBER
  years?

8. Are the students _____? Or do they lie around feeling _____
                  ADJ                      ADJ
  and _____?
      ADJ

9. And finally, college should be your _____. Make your choice
                                ADJ
  _____.
  ADJ

# Tips for Success in College

1. Don't talk to _____ about SAT scores; instead, ask about
        NOUN

   _____.
   PL. NOUN

2. Before registering for classes, ask some _____ which
                                            PL. NOUN

   professors are _____.
                   SUPER. ADJ

3. You don't want to get up too _____, so plan _____ your
                                 ADV            NOUN

   _____.
   ADV

4. Find out which _____, fraternities, or _____
                  COLL. NOUN                   SUPER. ADJ

   have the _____ parties.
            COLL. NOUN

5. Some places to study are _____ than others. Shop
                            COMP. ADJ

   around.

6. Remember, _____ are not as important as _____.
             PL. NOUN                        PL. NOUN

## How to Go On a Job Interview

1. Do some research so that you'll _____ be able to _____.
                                    VERB              ADV

2. Make sure you wear your _____; looking _____ is important.
                            NOUN            ADJ

3. Check to see that you don't have _____ between your teeth,
                                     NOUN
   and that your hair looks _____ and your clothes are _____
                             ADJ                        ADJ
   and _____.
        ADJ

4. Comport yourself in a _____ manner.
                          ADJ

5. When you meet the interviewer, shake _____  _____
                                         PL. NOUN    ADJ
   and smile.

6. Try not to look _____; remember that the interviewer is a
                    ADJ
   _____ too. (Imaging him without his _____ on.)
    NOUN                                 PL. NOUN

7. Finally, just be _____, and if that doesn't _____, just
                     REFL. PRO                      VERB
   be someone else.

# The Sentence

The sentence is the primary unit of grammar, and understanding the sentence is the key to good grammar. Try to think of it as fluid and malleable, and as expressive of the information you're communicating, of the orderliness of your thinking, and of your personality. Your syntax, which is simply the structure of your sentences, tells your audience something about how your mind works—you don't want your message to be that the lights are on but nobody's home.

# Basic Elements Of The Sentence

The sentence is made up of two basic parts: the subject and the predicate. The predicate may be simple or it may be extremely complicated; this chapter shows you how to separate subject from predicate, and how to break the predicate down into its component parts: phrases, clauses, and objects. In Part 1, you learned parts of speech, and those lessons still apply here. Instead of looking at the functions of single words, you'll be looking at the functions of longer and longer groups of words.

# A. The Subject

The subject of a sentence is the main noun (the noun doing the action), along with any words or phrases that modify the main noun. The main noun by itself is called the simple subject. Every sentence has a subject, although sometimes the subject is implied. To find the subject of a sentence, first find the main verb. Then ask yourself, Who or what is doing this action? Below are some examples of subjects, which are italicized.

*My dog* has three legs. (Who has? *My dog.*)

After tonight, *Wanda* will never speak to Ralph again.
(who will never speak? *Wanda.*)

*Wanda and Max* left the office at midnight.
(Who left? *Wanda and Max.*)

Obviously, *the election* is over. (What is over? *The election.*)

Get lost! (Who should get lost? The implied subject is *you.*)

---

### Quick Quiz #15
### Finding the Subject

*Find the simple subject in the following sentences.*

1. Oscar saw a Martian sitting on a bench eating a banana.
2. Don't walk on the grass.
3. Who could live without ice cream?
4. Those socks have been under the bed for three weeks.
5. The roommates, after much discussion, finally bought a new sofa.

---

# Rules For Subjects

1. The subject and verb must agree in number. This means that a singular subject takes a singular verb, and a plural subject takes a plural verb. You don't have to be able to distinguish singular verbs from plural verbs; you do have to distinguish between singular and plural subjects. Why? Because if you can determine whether a subject is singular or plural, your ear will be able to match it with the correct verb. If your subject is singular, match the verb with *it;* if your subject is plural, use *they.* See Part 3, Section A for more explanation and practice.

2. Bracketing prepositional phrases may help you find the subject.

Six [of the men] [with beards] wore only one shoe.

(verb: *wore;* subject: *six*)

[On Tuesday] people [with dogs] [on leashes] meet [in the park].

(verb: *meet;* subject: *people)*

---

## Quick Quiz #16

### Billy Wifflamoo, Teen Love Idol

*Locate each verb and circle it. Underline the subject of each verb, and draw a line connecting the two.*

There came a moment (and a short moment it was) when Billy was the primary love object of all the girls in his school. Girls had been falling for the best-looking, most athletic, most charming boys, but one day, Billy had something none of them had: he had actual contact with an alien. This made him famous and much admired.

The alien had touched Billy's ear with his spiky green finger. Billy's ear had swelled to six times the normal size for ears, and he was suddenly able to hear very acutely. He could hear what his neighbors were saying in their living room, which was not at all interesting. The alien touched all of Billy's body parts, and in turn, each grew to six times its normal size. Soon Billy himself was a pretty big guy. The alien taught Billy how to do this for himself, whenever he felt like it. He performed this trick at school, which was why the girls fell in love with him. It didn't last.

After Billy shrank back to normal size, he and the alien talked about baseball. The alien liked the Red Sox, a doomed team if ever there was one.

---

# B. The Predicate

The predicate is the part of the sentence that isn't the subject. The verb is part of the predicate, as well as everything else in the sentence—phrases, direct and indirect objects—that is not part of the subject. Explained another way, the predicate *says* something about the subject.

| Subject | Predicate |
|---------|-----------|
| Wanda | was greedy. |
| She | loved money more than anything else. |

**Possible Confusion:** The subject more often comes first in a sentence, and putting the subject first is probably the more straightforward way to organize a sentence. But for variety, and even for suspense, writers can choose to reverse the order, putting the predicate first and the subject last, or putting parts of the predicate on either side of the subject. The foolproof way to find the subject is to first locate the verb, and then to ask yourself who or what is doing this action?

> Through the imposing gateway came Wanda, determined to impress everyone and everything in her path.

The verb is *came*. Who came? *Wanda* came. Wanda is the subject; everything else is the predicate. See how the predicate is saying something *about* Wanda?

> There were thousands of candy wrappers on the floor.

The verb is *were*. What *were* on the floor? *Thousands of candy wrappers. Thousands of candy wrappers* is the subject; everything else is the predicate. *There* is never the subject of a sentence; if a sentence begins with *there,* look for the subject to come after the verb.

Why is this important? **A sentence must have a subject and a predicate.** If you're missing either part, you don't have a sentence. Obviously, as any playwright or screenwriter knows, we don't speak in complete sentences. And many advertisements are nothing more than strings of sentence fragments, even single words followed by a period. Fine. But when you're writing formally, you must write in complete sentences. And even if you're writing informally, it helps to know what rules you're breaking.

# C. Predicate: The Sequel

Let's look at a simple sentence and see how far we can go with it, by complicating the predicate.

Wanda walked.

*Wanda* is the subject; *walked* is the predicate, the verb telling what Wanda did. Let's dress up our sentence with an adverb.

Wanda walked *quickly*.

So far, so good. Let's dress it up even more with a group of words, called a phrase.

Wanda walked quickly *to the beach.*

*Wanda* is still the subject; the predicate is *walked quickly to the beach.* The predicate now includes the verb *walked,* the adverb *quickly*, and the prepositional phrase *to the beach*, which tells where Wanda walked.

We can add even more prepositional phrases.

*In a snit,* Wanda walked quickly *with a towel to the beach.*

The prepositional phrases are: *In a snit, with a towel, to the beach.* These phrases further describe Wanda and what she was doing. Now, let's really go wild.

*Because she was in a snit,* Wanda walked quickly with a towel to the beach, *which was deserted after the weather service announced an impending tidal wave.*

The subject is still *Wanda;* the predicate is everything else, including the clauses *Because she was in a snit, which was deserted,* and *after the weather service announced an impending tidal wave.* Remember that the predicate's job is to tell something about the subject. See how adding to the predicate told us more and more about Wanda and her walking?

The predicate may be full of all kinds of descriptions, modifiers, and extra information such as direct and indirect objects—or the predicate may be quite simple: an undecorated, lonely verb. Let's look closely at some of these elements of the predicate.

# The Direct Object

The direct object is not the subject of the sentence, it is the noun receiving the action. A sentence doesn't need a direct object to be a sentence. Instead of doing something, the direct object has something done *to* it.

Wanda threw the flowers.

*Wanda* is the subject; she's the one doing the throwing. *Flowers* is the object; they aren't doing anything, but something is being done to them—they are being thrown.

Max loved *money.*
(What did Max love? *Money* is the direct object.)

Thelma and Louise robbed a *store* and stole a *car.*
(What did they rob? A *store.* What did they steal? A *car.*)

# The Indirect Object

You need a direct object to have an indirect object. An indirect object is really an understood prepositional phrase. For example:

Wanda threw Max the flowers. (*flowers* is the direct object; *Max* is the indirect object)

**Or:** Wanda threw the flowers to Max. (*flowers* is the direct object; *to Max* is a prepositional phrase)

Marlene gave *him* a dog biscuit. (*him* is the indirect object)

Tell *me* a riddle. (*me* is the indirect object)

# D. Phrases

A phrase is a group of words that acts as a part of speech rather than as a complete sentence. You already know the function of a noun, adjective, or adverb—a phrase merely takes on one of those functions. A phrase does not have a subject and a verb. The two main kinds of phrases are prepositional phrases and verbal phrases.

## Prepositional Phrases

By far the most common kind of phrase is the prepositional phrase, which begins, incredibly, with a preposition, and ends with a noun. (See Prepositions, Part 1, Section F.) Let's return to our sentence.

Because she was in a snit, Wanda walked quickly with a towel to the beach.

Again, the prepositional phrases are *in a snit, with a towel,* and *to the beach.* Let's look at what these phrases are doing in the sentence.

*in a snit* describes Wanda, so *in a snit* is an adjective phrase.

*with a towel* also describes Wanda; it, too, is an adjective phrase.

*to the beach* describes where Wanda walked, so it is an adverb phrase.

All of these phrases are still prepositional phrases, and prepositional phrases usually act either as adjectives or adverbs. Occasionally a prepositional phrase acts as a noun.

*Before dinner* is a good time to do homework.
(*Before dinner* is the subject of *is*)

## Quick Quiz #19

### Finding Prepositional Phrases

*Bracket the prepositional phrases. Notice that without the prepositional phrases, you still have a sentence that can stand by itself.*

1. In a huff, Deidre marched to the party.

2. Her boyfriend, in a new suit, stood out in the crowd.

3. Many of the partygoers wore socks on their hands.

4. Deidre could see a couple kissing across the room.

5. Beyond the kissing couple she noticed a table heaped with a pile of socks, and under the table was a stack of CDs.

# Verbals

Another kind of phrase is the verbal—infinitives, gerunds, and participles. As you can tell from the name, they are related to verbs. They looked verby, but never act as verbs. Instead they act as nouns, adjectives, or adverbs. Let's look at the three types.

# Infinitive Phrases

When the preposition *to* is followed by a noun, it is a prepositional phrase: *to the beach.* When *to* is followed by a verb—*to run, to see, to feel*—it is an infinitive. Why does this matter? The rules that govern infinitives are different from the rules that govern prepositional phrases; also, since infinitives are closely related to verbs, they can have a passive or active voice as well be in the present or perfect tense.

Wanda wanted *to leave.*
(What did Wanda want? *To leave,*
an infinitive phrase acting as a noun.)

He works hard *to make money.*
(Why does he work? *to make money,* an infinitive phrase
acting as a adverb, modifying *work.*)

*To read is to be transported* to another world.
(*To read* is an infinitive acting as a noun, and the subject of *is; to be transported* is an infinitive acting as a noun, the object of *is; to another world* is a prepositional phrase acting as an adverb, telling *where transported.*) (Whew!)

To play around with the infinitives we've already used, let's change them slightly.

Wanda wanted *to have left.*
(*to have left* is an infinitive phrase, perfect tense)

*To have read* is *to have been transported* to another world.
(*to have read* is a perfect infinitive phrase; *to have been transported* is a perfect passive infinitive phrase)

**A Moment of Reassurance:** No one, except maybe your grammar teacher, is ever going to ask you to identify a perfect passive infinitive phrase. So relax. What is important is being able to identify the parts of the sentence, including the subject and verb. Sometimes the subject of the sentence is not anything as simple as *I* or *Wanda*—it might be something more complicated, like *To have read.* Don't worry too much about the details, but be able to spot an infinitive when you see one, whether it is passive or active, present or perfect.

## Quick Quiz #20

### Finding Infinitives

*Bracket the infinitive phrases.*

1. When Deirdre saw her boyfriend, she wanted to scream.

2. She talked to her friend Bob, who wanted to be told why everyone was wearing socks on their hands.

3. Deirdre wanted to know why her boyfriend was such a cad.

4. To have been in love is to have suffered.

5. She needed to find him and to hold his sock-covered hand.

# Gerund Phrases

A gerund is an *-ing* verb that acts as a noun. Since it acts as a noun, it can be the subject of a sentence or the object of a verb or preposition.

> *Daydreaming* was her favorite pastime.

> *Winning the lottery* is my only hope.

> She loved *eating pastries* and *staying up all night.*

Use ownership words instead of subject or object pronouns before a gerund.

> *Mark's* leaving caused a great stir.
>
> Not: *Mark* leaving caused a great stir.

> Wanda was ecstatic about *his* choosing her as his successor.
>
> Not: Wanda was ecstatic about *him* choosing her as his successor.

---

## Quick Quiz #21

### Finding Gerunds

*Circle the gerunds below. Note that they always perform the function of a noun.*

1. Bob hated cleaning.

2. Partying and talking on the phone took up most of his time.

3. He was thinking of hiring someone to clean his apartment but unfortunately, spending money was another thing he hated.

# Participial Phrases

These are simply phrases that have verbs but not subjects. A participle is really half of a verb.

| past participle | verb | present participle |
|---|---|---|
| fallen | had fallen | falling |
| screaming | was screaming | screaming |

See the difference? A participle can't take a subject, because it's missing part of the verb. A participle looks like a verb, but it isn't complete.

The function of a participial phrase is to modify a noun—in other words, a participial phrase acts as an adjective.

*Had* or *have plus* a past participle gives you a verb in the past perfect tense. *Is* or *are* plus a present participle gives you a verb in present progressive. But by itself, a participle isn't a complete verb. It can, however, act as an adjective.

*Lying on her bed,* Wanda ordered Chinese food.

*Screaming with laughter,* the secretaries hid under their desks.

Dolores, *left behind at the office,* wept over her spreadsheets.

The socks *lost in the dryer* were her favorites.

See how each participial phrase tells us something about a noun? *Lying on her bed* describes Wanda, *screaming with laughter* describes the secretaries, and *lost in the dryer* describes the socks. Notice that *Wanda* is the subject of the verb *ordered*; secretaries is the subject of *hid*; socks is the subject of *were*. So *lying, screaming, left,* and *lost* have no subject; instead of acting as verbs, they are describing the subject of the sentence. Recognizing participial phrases is crucial in avoiding the dreaded misplaced modifier or dangling participle. See Part 3, Section C.

## Quick Quiz #22

### Identifying Participial Phrases

*Bracket the participial phrases in the following sentences. Remember that the function of a participial phrase is to modify a noun or pronoun.*

1. Walking quickly to work, Bob realized he was wearing only one shoe.

2. Too tired to turn back, he thought that maybe his co-workers would think he was on the cutting edge of fashion.

3. His desk, covered with piles of papers and pone messages, was the only safe place.

4. Throwing himself into his work, he forgot about his missing shoe, and wandered out into the hallway for a drink of water.

5. Laughing and pointing, Bob's colleagues gathered around to stare at his naked foot.

# E. Clauses

Clauses are like phrases, but with one big difference. A clause has a subject and a verb, a phrase does not. Clauses fall into two categories: independent and dependent.

An independent clause can stand by itself as a whole, complete sentence. A dependent (or subordinate) clause, on the other hand, is *dependent* on the rest of the sentence; it can't stand by itself. Let's look at some examples.

Wanda wore the dress that she had bought on Tuesday.

What's the subject? *Wanda.* What's the predicate? *wore the dress that she had bought on Tuesday.*

So far so good. Notice that our predicate has two verbs in it—one of them, *wore*, has *Wanda* as its subject. The other, *had bought*, has *she* as its subject. Two clauses, each with a subject and a verb. Which clause can stand by itself?

Wanda wore the dress.

That she had bought on Tuesday.

The first clause is independent—it looks and feels like a sentence, doesn't it? The second clause is dependent—it needs to be attached to the other clause; it can't stand by itself.

How do you tell the difference? A dependent clause will be introduced either by a relative pronoun (*that, which, who*) or a lining conjunction (*after, although, as, because, before, if, since, unless, until, when, while*).

### Rule For Dependent Clauses

Be careful not to try to pass off a dependent clause as a complete sentence unless you are writing informally or you are doing it intentionally for emphasis. A dependent clause that is not attached to an independent clause is called a sentence fragment, and nothing drives teachers and professors crazier than sloppy, unintended sentence fragments.

### More On Dependent Clauses

A dependent clause can have a variety of functions. It can act as an adjective: *that she had bought on Tuesday* describes the dress, which make it an adjective clause. Dependent clauses can also function as nouns or adverbs.

# Noun Clauses

Below are some examples of noun clauses.

I can't explain *what he did.* (*what he did* is the object of *explain*)

*Whoever broke the lamp* must pay for it.
(*Whoever bore the lamp* is the subject of *must pay*)

Bob realized *that he was a clumsy ox.*
(*that he was a clumsy ox* is the object of *realized*)

### Rules For Noun Clauses

1. A noun clause generally goes after the verb; however, if the clause is the subject of the sentence, it may begin the sentence.

2. A noun clause may function in a sentence any way that a noun functions; that is, it may be the subject of a verb, or the object of a verb or preposition.

3. Noun clauses are usually introduced by *that.* They may also be introduced by *what, which, who, whom, where, when, whoever, whatever.*

# Adjective Clauses

Below are some examples of adjective clauses.

The lamp, *which was a priceless heirloom*, lay smashed on the floor.
(*which was a priceless heirloom* modifies *lamp*)

Bob leaned over to gather up the glass *that was on the rug.*
(*that was on the rug* modifies *glass*)

Bob went to see the woman *who owned the lamp.*
(*who owned the lamp* modifies *woman*)

## Rules For Adjective Clauses

1. Put an adjective clause right after the noun it modifies; otherwise, it may be unclear what is being modified. Look back at the adjective clause examples. See how nothing comes between the noun and modifying clause?

2. Adjective clauses begin with the relative pronouns *who, whom, whose, which,* or *that.* Another name for a adjective clause is a relative clause—you can think of it as a clause *related* to the noun it modifies.

# Adverb Clauses

Below are some examples of adverb clauses.

Bob felt sick *when she told him the value of the lamp.*
(*when she told him the value of the lamp* tells when Bob felt sick,
so it modifies the verb *felt*)

*If he had known how much the lamp was worth,* he would have
been more careful. (the clause modifies *would have been*)

He was in more trouble *than he ever thought possible.*
(the clause modifies *more*)

## Rules For Adverb Clauses

1. Put adverb clauses right before or right after the independent
   clause. Avoid ambiguity.

2. **Adverb** clauses may be introduced by *when, before, after, until,
   since, while, where, when, as, as if, because, although, while,
   if, unless, so, so that.* Adverb clauses, just like adverbs, modify
   verbs, adjectives, or other adverbs. Adverb clauses tend to
   explain *when, where, how,* and *if.*

**Word of Reassurance:** You do not have to memorize the introductory
words for the various types of clauses. You do have to be able to
spot a dependent clause when you see one, and to understand the
distinction between independent and dependent clauses.

**Word of Warning:** If you write essays full of dependent clauses that
begin with capital letters and end in periods, you will not impress
your teacher. You will be marked as a Sentence Fragmenter, you will
get low grades, and you will not have glory in your academic life.
Not good.

The functions of clauses are exactly the same as the parts of speech functions you have already learned. If you are having a great deal of trouble with this, go back to Part 1 and review parts of speech, particularly noun, adjective, and adverb. The same functions apply to clauses; the only difference is that clauses are strings of words instead of only one word.

## Quick Quiz #23

### Identifying Dependent Clauses

*In each of the following sentences, place parentheses around the dependent clause and label it as a noun, adjective, or adverb clause.*

1. When the party was assembled at the table, Rocky raised his glass and called for a toast, and everyone gleefully threw pieces of toast at him.

2. The wedding, which was scheduled to take place at midnight, had been called off 16 times so far.

3. What made the couple so uncertain was not entirely clear to those at the party.

4. Because the wedding was to be held at midnight, some of the older guests began nodding off during dessert.

5. After they had eaten, the bride and groom drew mustaches on the sleeping guests.

# Summary

- **Subject:** The word or group of words that is doing the action of the verb. You must have a subject, or an implied subject, to have a sentence. Find the subject by first finding the verb, and then asking yourself, who or what is doing this action? (*Reginald* danced; *Dancing* is fun; Where are *you*?)

- **Predicate:** The part of a sentence that is not the subject. The predicate includes the verb and any words or phrases modifying the verb. (The boys *were dancing on the roof. In the moonlight* they *looked like ghosts.*)

- **Phrase:** A group of words. A phrase does not have a subject and a verb.

- **Prepositional Phrase:** A group of words that bgins with a preposition and ends

- **Verbal:** A phrase that acts a noun, adjective, or adverb. A verbal looks like a verb but doesn't act as a verb. The three kinds of verbal phrases are gerunds, infinitives, and participles.

- **Gerund:** A gerund always ends in *-ing,* and always acts as noun. (*Running* is tiring; His *complaining* gets on my nerves.)

- **Infinitive:** The verb form that begins with *to.* Infinitives can act as nouns, adjectives, or adverbs. (to run; to think; to have; to have been creeping)

- **Participial Phrase:** The present participle is the *-ing* form of the verb (is sneezing; was sleeping). The past participle goes with *have*, and usually ends in *-ed* (have *sneezed*; have *danced*). A participle is the *-ing* or *-ed* part of the verb without its helper (sneezing, sleeping, sneezed, danced, slept). A participial phrase always acts as an adjective.

- **Clause:** A group of words that has a subject and a verb. Clauses can act as nouns, adjectives, or adverbs.

- **Independent Clause:** A clause that can stand by itself as a sentence. (*The man fell* and *the lamp broke.* Because he was crazy, *the man laughed at adversity.*)

- **Dependent Clause:** A clause that can't stand by itself as a sentence. Dependent clauses are also called subordinate clauses, and they may act as nouns, adjectives, or adverbs. (*Because he was crazy,* the man laughed at adversity. Pull up your pants *before you leave the house.* The woman *who wrote the book* has six toes.)

# PART 3

# Putting It All Together

# A. Agreement

Examples from the Masters:

*A writer is like a bean plant—he has his little day, and then get stringy.*

–E.B. White

*The future is something which everyone reaches at the rate of sixty minutes and hour, whatever her does, whoever he is.*

–C.S. Lewis

Let's do some analysis. In the first quote, *writer* is the singular subject, *is* is the singular verb. *He* is a singular pronoun, to match *writer* (it's a little sexist, but more on that later.) *Has* and *gets* are singular verbs to match the singular pronoun. Everything is singular and everything matches.

In the second quote, *future* is the singular subject, matching the singular verb *is*. *Everyone* is singular, matching the singular verb *reaches* and the singular pronoun *he*. *Does* and *is* are also singular, to match *he*.

All of that analysis just explains why the sentences sound right—agreement doesn't attract any attention unless it is wrong.

In the contest for Most Popular Error, agreement is probably the big winner. There are two kinds of agreement you need to watch out for: subject-verb agreement and pronoun agreement. We've mentioned each of these earlier in the sections on subjects, nouns, and pronouns, but let's go into more detail about these agreements.

# Subject-Verb Agreement

---

### The Rule
Singular subjects take singular verbs, and plural subjects take plural verbs.

---

# Four Easy Steps For Avoiding Subject-Verb Embarrassment

1. Find the main verb. Don't be distracted by verbals, which are verb-like elements acting as another part of speech (infinitives, gerunds or participles as you read about in Part 2).

2. Ask yourself: Who or what is doing this action? The answer to this question will be the subject. The subject does not necessarily come before the verb, and there may be all kinds of distracting modifiers and prepositional phrases in between the subject and the verb. Do not lose heart. Bracketing such phrases so that you can see the subject more clearly may help.

3. Is the subject singular or plural? Most of the time, a plural subject will end in -s; there are plenty of exceptions. You may also have to consider the intended meaning of the word. (See Rules for Nouns, pages 16.)

4. If your subject is singular, match *it* with the correct verb. If your subject is plural, match *they* with the correct verb. We promise you will be able to conjugate this correctly, by using your ear.

### Subject-Verb Olympics

*For the bronze, circle the appropriate verb form.*

1. Wearing a clown outfit, Bob (were sitting, was sitting) in a tire swing.

2. Bob, distracted by daydreams, (is, are) eating Doritos and licking his fingers.

3. Many of the causes of gaining weight (is, are) unknown to Bob.

4. The danger of eating too many chips (do, does) not worry him.

5. The dangers of eating too many chips (do, does) not worry him.

# Rules For Subject-Verb Agreement

1. Subjects connected by *and* are plural: Bob *and* Dick *are* here.

2. Certain expressions (*as well as, including, together with, with,* etc. logically seem to change a singular subject to plural. They don't These expressions will be set off from the subject by commas.

   Bob, *along with* Dick and Harry, *is going* on vacation.

   Dick, *as well* as Bob, *plans* to vacation in his living room.

3. Singular subjects connected by conjunctions such as *either-or, neither-nor, or,* and *nor* stay singular.

   *Neither* Bob *nor* Harry *is* able to get up from the Barcalounger.

4. If a singular and plural subject are connected by *either-or, neither-nor, or,* or *nor* the verb should agree with the subject closest to it.

> Neither Bob nor *the others were* able to get up from the Barcalounger.

> Neither the others nor *Bob was* able to get up from the Barcalounger.

---

## Quick Quiz #25

### Subject-Verb Olympics

*For the silver, circle the appropriate verb form:*

1. To the naked eye, Bob and Harry (look, looks) too fat to get up from the Barcalounger.

2. Dick, together with Harry, (is yearning, are yearning) for some ice cream.

3. Either Bob or Dick (want, wants) nuts and fudge to go with the ice cream.

4. Neither the boys nor Bob (desire, desires) green vegetables.

5. Neither Bob nor the boys (desire, desires) green vegetables.

---

## Even More Rules For Subject-Verb Agreement

1. *There* is never the subject of a sentence. Look for the subject to follow the verb: There *are* many *reasons* to sit in a tire swing.

2. Be careful with relative pronouns *who, which,* and *that.* Look to see which non the relative pronoun is standing in for, and make your verb appropriately singular or plural to match it.

*Ladies* who *lunch* on Tuesdays eat vichyssoise.
A *lady* who *lunches* on Tuesday eats vichyssoise.

Bob is one of the *men* who *eat* tortilla chips before dinner.
Bob is one *man* who *eats* tortilla chips before dinner.

Note that *Ladies* is the subject of *eat*; *Bob* is the subject of *is*. The italicized noun is the antecedent for *who*, showing whether *who* should be considered singular or plural. More examples of this tricky rule are on the next page.

A hammer is one of the *tools* that *are* indispensable.

At the hardware store, Bob looked at *rakes* that *were* on sale.

This rake is the only *one* of all these tools that *is* made by Acme Tools.

Again, note that the italicized noun is not the subject of the italicized verb; the subject of the italicized verb is the relative pronoun *that*. The italicized noun is the noun that *that* stands for. At issue here is the meaning of the sentence—if, in the last example, the writer intends to say that out of all the tools, the rake is the only tool made by Acme, then the subject-verb agreement is correct as it stands. If the writer means that all of the tools are made by Acme, then the subject-verb agreement (and the sentence as a whole) makes no sense. Be clear about what you want say, and use subject-verb agreement to say what you mean.

3. Collective nouns such as *family, committee, jury, crowd,* and *group* are almost always singular. (See Rules for Nouns, page 16.)

4. Numbers that represent a single unit are singular.

*A million dollars is* a lot of money to keep under your mattress.

*Fifty percent is* a big commission.

*Ten years is* a long time to be without work.

# Pronoun Agreement

This is not as complicated as subject-verb agreement; once you know the rule, it's just a matter of not being sloppy.

---

### The Rule

Use a singular pronoun with a singular antecedent; use a plural pronoun with a plural antecedent.

---

Remember that the antecedent is the word a pronoun stands in for in a sentence—the noun the pronoun is referring to. If the antecedent is singular, the pronoun should be singular; if the antecedent is plural, the pronoun should be plural.

*Bob and Harry* are eating *their* tortilla chips.

*Neither* Bob nor Harry is eating *his* tortilla chips.

*Each* of the men is eating *his* tortilla chips.

*Everyone* should eat *his* pizza.

*Everyone* should eat *her* pizza.

**Not:** *Everyone* should eat *their* pizza.

Sometimes the application of this rule can get you into an awkward spot.

When a man or a woman falls in love, he becomes absent-minded.

What about the woman? The pronoun should logically include her as well, which is why some writer might fall for:

**Sloppy:** When a man or woman falls in love, they become absent-minded.

**Overly politically correct:** When a man or woman falls in love, he or she becomes absent-minded.

It's far better to rewrite as the following:

When men and women fall in love, they become absent-minded.

Now we're consistently plural. Remember: If sticking to a rule leaves you with an awkward sentence, rewrite! Keep in mind the Golden Rule of Grammar.

---

## The Golden Rule
Avoid trouble.

---

# Last Words On Pronoun Agreement

1. Be consistent in your use of pronouns. Do this:

   *You* must pick up *your* ticket before taking *your* seat.

   **Not:** *One* must pick up *one's* ticket before taking *your* seat.

   This inconsistency most often comes up with *one* and *you*. Be careful to maintain consistency, or it will look like you suffered memory loss between starting your sentence and ending it.

2. Nouns connected to singular pronouns should also be singular; nouns connected to plural pronouns should be plural. For example:

   Each of the men asked for a raise.

   **Not:** Each of the men asked for raises.

   All of the men wore dresses.

   **Not:** All of the men wore a dress.

   See the confusion stirred up by the violation of this rule? In the latter example, the second version says that all of the men were wearing the same dress. All at the same time? Again, one of the best reasons for understanding the rules of grammar is that you can avoid giving your sentences unintended meanings.

3. Make sure that the noun your pronoun refers to is obvious.

   Ralphie and Marky fell down, and *he* broke his leg.

   Who broke his leg? We aren't sure. This is an obvious example; in a more complicated sentence either the reader will be confused (never a good thing) or she will make an arbitrary decision about what the pronoun refers to (not good either). Check pronouns to see if their antecedents are clear.

   Another kind of ambiguity crops up most often in the use of pointing (or demonstrative) pronouns.

Liberty has been defined as freedom limited by whatever causes harm to others, and this is how a person tries to live a moral life.

You more or less understand the writer's point—but what, exactly, does *this* refer to? *Liberty? Limited freedom?* The intended antecedent is *living freely without causing harm to others,* but since that phrase is not in the sentence, the reader is left with the job of assigning an antecedent to the pronoun. Watch out for *this, that, these,* and *those.* Don't ask the reader to do work that you should be doing.

## Quick Quiz #27

### Pronoun Agreement

*Correct the pronoun agreement in the following sentences. Not every sentence has an error.*

1. In an election year, many of the candidates abandon their usual causes and talk instead about any issue he thinks will get him elected.

2. Unfortunately, a campaign manager will do virtually anything, legal or not, to ensure their candidate's reelection.

3. Each of the voters makes their own decisions.

4. Everyone in the campaign office has, at one time or another, offered a suggestion for an advertisement that would severely damage the opposing candidate's credibility, but each person has since retracted their suggestion, fearing that such an advertisement would invite attacks on their own candidate's credibility.

5. It is a fact of politics that our votes are based, finally, on the most subjective measures, and that a politician's hairstyle may hurt his chances more than his positions on policy or even his voting record.

# B. Parallel Construction

Examples from the Masters:

*Let every nation know, whether it wishes us well or ill, that we shall pay any price, bear any burden, meet any hardship, support any friend, oppose any foe to assure the survival and the success of liberty.*

–John F. Kennedy

*To be a woman is to have the same needs and longings as a man.*

–Liv Ullmann

Let's do some analysis. The first example is a *series,* and each element in the series is equal in form to the others. Kennedy says we shall, *pay, bear, meet, support,* and *oppose.* Five verbs. The final example is a kind of equals sign: Liv Ullmann says *To be = to have.* Two infinitives.

Balance, symmetry, consistency. Parallel construction gives your writing elegance and logic.

---

### The Rule
Sentences, or parts of sentences that are connected by idea, should be expressed in similar form.

---

The elements in the series may be **nouns.**

In analyzing the value of a company, Wanda paid attention to the *amount* of debt, the underlying *assets,* and the *prospects* for growth.

**Not:** In analyzing the value of a company, Wanda paid attention to the *amount* of debt, the underlying *assets,* and *whether* the company had prospects for growth.

What did Wanda pay attention to? A list of three nouns: *amount, assets,* and *prospects.* Each noun has additional modifiers—the prepositional phrases *of debt* and *for growth,* and the adjective *underlying.* The errant example makes a list of two nouns and a clause.

Or the elements in the series may be **phrases.**

Wanda wanted *to make* a lot of money, *buy* stock, and *retire* early.

**Not:** Wanda wanted *to make* a lot of money, *buy* stock, and *she wanted* to retire early.

In this case Wanda wanted to do three things: *to make, to buy,* and *to retire*—three infinitive phrases. *A lot of money* and *stock* are objects of the infinitive, and *early* is an adverb. Note that the *to* may be dropped after the first element; it is understood to carry through to the other two infinitives. The errant example makes a list of two infinitive phrases and a clause.

Or the elements in the series may be **clauses.**

Wanda believed *that* a healthy portfolio was a necessity, *that* the only way to live was to work hard and play hard, and *that* knowledge was power.

**Not:** Wanda believed *that* a health portfolio was a necessity, *that* the only way to live was to work hard and play hard, and *in gaining* power through knowledge.

Here the sentence is more complicated, but it is still composed of a list—a list of three things Wanda believed. Each element is a subordinate clause, with its own subject and verb, and none of the elements can exist alone as a sentence. The errant example makes a list of two subordinate clauses and one phrase containing the gerund *gaining.*

Notice that it is helpful to ignore adjectives, adverbs, and prepositional phrases when you are looking at the composition of the sentence. Finding the part of speech of the elements in the list is easier when you look at the sentence without the dressing of modifiers.

1. If your sentence has seesaw, or correlative, conjunctions (*either/or, neither/nor, not only/but also, both/and, whether/or*), make sure you match the parts on either side. It's a little like keeping a seesaw balanced: whatever you have on one side of the conjunction, you must match in form on the other side. Think consistency.

She stayed up late *either working* at the office *or going* to parties

**Not:** She stayed up late *either working* at the office *or she would go* to parties.

Unlike her colleagues, Wanda had an ambition *not only to succeed* at work *but also to impress* the entire city with the force of her personality.

**Not:** Unlike her colleagues, Wanda had an ambition *not only to succeed* at work *but also wanted* to impress the entire city with the force of her personality.

2. If the elements in your series are preceded by a preposition or an article, you can leave out the preposition or article after the first element, as long as you leave it out for good.

On her first visit to Paris she was delighted *with the sound* of people speaking French, *with the grandeur* of the architecture, and *with the delicious feeling* of being away from home.

**Or:** On her first visit to Paris she was delighted *with the sound* of people speaking French, *the grandeur* of the architecture, and *the delicious feeling* of being away from home.

**Not:** On her first visit to Paris she was delighted *with the sound* of people speaking French, *the grandeur* of the architecture, and *with the delicious feeling* of being away from home.

# Embarrassing Moments In Parallel Construction

Harvard Business School ran the following ad:

> *What's innovative, time-tested, diverse, intense, global, and develop leaders?*

If you winced at Harvard's list of adjective-adjective-adjective-adjective-adjective-VERB—then the rule of parallel construction has begun to sink in. (And let's not forget, Harvard no longer requires its Business School applicants to take the GMAT, which has a whole section devoted to grammar. Hmm. What do we make of this?)

Now take a look at a warning printed on the side of many cigarette packages—a warning seen by millions of smokers.

> *Smoking Causes Lung Cancer, Heart Disease, Emphysema, and May Complicate Pregnancy.*

The series is a list of nouns: lung cancer, heart disease, emphysema, may complicate—oops, *may complicate* is no noun. The sentence is constructed to say that *smoking causes may complicate*. Which clearly makes no sense at all. These smokers are not only buying a product that is bad for their health but also getting a lesson a bad grammar. (See, parallel construction at work with correlative conjunctions? Not only *buying*...but also *getting*.)

## Parallel Construction

*Pick the best answer.*

1. Wanda, unlike the others in her office, yearned to take on extra responsibilities such as writing reports, <u>managing newly hired workers, and to plan</u> brainstorming sessions, and analyzing every twist and turn of the market.

   A) managing newly hired workers, and to plan
   B) managing newly hired workers, for planning
   C) to manage newly hired workers for the planning of
   D) to manage workers that were newly hired, and to plan
   E) managing newly hired workers, planning

2. Wanda's suspicion that Max was involved in some kind of shady deal <u>sprang not from any particular incident but developed</u> over a long period of observation.

   A) sprang not from any particular incident but developed
   B) sprang not from any particular incident but rather developed
   C) was not springing from any particular incident but developing
   D) did not spring from any particular incident but developed
   E) did not spring from any incident particular but was developing

3. She imagined that Max used his weekends to sneak into the office, to go through files, <u>to communicate with the opposition, and for planning his next move</u>.

   A) to communicate with the opposition, and for planning his next move
   B) to communicate with the opposition, and to plan his next move
   C) to communicate with the opposition, planning his next move
   D) for communicating with the opposition, and for planning his next move
   E) for communicating with the opposition so as to plan his next move

4. Wanda hoped that she would be the one to uncover Max's disloyalty, <u>and figure out a way to spy on the spy himself</u>, and that by her wily efforts she would earn a promotion and a hefty raise.

A) and figure out a way to spy on the spy himself
B) that she would figure out a way to spy on the spy himself
C) that by figuring out a way to spy on the spy himself
D) by her figuring out a way for her to be spying on the spy himself
E) thereby figuring out a way for spying on him, the spy

5. After many sleepless nights, she decided to research companies that specialize in high-tech surveillance techniques, which would allow her to get incriminating evidence <u>by bugging his phone, and to make</u> friends with his secretary so that she could get access to his office without arousing suspicion.

A) by bugging his phone, and to make
B) by bugging his phone, and by making
C) by bugging his phone, and she would make
D) from bugging his and from making
E) to bug his phone, and to make

# C. Misplaced Modifiers

Examples from the Masters:

*For all her chic thinness, she had an almost breakfast-cereal air of health, a soap and lemon cleanness, a rough pink darkening in the cheeks.*

–Truman Capote, *Breakfast at Tiffany's*

*Thinking finally of the consequences, he fell to dreaming as the last horse, a yearling running at an angle, job-trotted into the corral to drink in the creek alongside the other shadowy horses deployed as regularly as a picket line.*

–Thomas McGuane, *Nobody's Angel*

What is remarkable about these sentences? Well, they're a pleasure to read, and their modifiers aren't misplaced. In Capote's sentence, *For all her chic thinness* is describing someone: *she.* The noun being modified follows the modifier, so there is no confusion.

In McGuane's sentence, who was *thinking finally of the consequences*? *He,* which immediately follows the modifier. McGuane has two correctly placed modifiers in his sentence. What were *deployed as regularly as a picket line*? The *horses.* Again, no confusion. Now let's look at what not to do.

Running at top speed, my wig flew off.

Here we have a participial phrase, *Running at top speed.* Remember that participial phrases always act as adjectives. Who or what is being described? *Wig* is the only noun in the sentence, and it is placed right next to the phrase. So the sentence is constructed to make our phrase modify *wig*, which, unless this is wacky science fiction, is not the intention of the writer. Fix it by changing the sentence to the following:

I was running at top speed when my wig flew off.

**Or:** As I was running at top speed, my wig flew off.

What we have done is supply a subject for *running at top speed*; we have turned the participial phrase into a clause, with its own subject and verb.

> **Or:** Running at top speed, I felt my wig fly off.

This time *running at top speed* is still a phrase, but what the phrase modifies comes right after the comma: *I*.

Check out the following examples:

> While I was eating my pizza, the phone rang.

> **Not:** While eating my pizza, the phone rang.

> The camera photographed the satellite hurtling through space.

> **Not:** Hurtling through space, the camera photographed the satellite.

> We had a fabulous time at the party, dancing and carousing until dawn.

> **Not:** The party was fabulous, dancing and carousing until dawn.

> To make a lot of money, you must work hard.

> **Not:** To make a lot of money, hard work is required.

Notice that all of these examples concern phrases—groups of words without subjects—and that the phrases cause confusion either because of their placement or because the thing being described is not actually mentioned in the sentence. The phone wasn't eating the pizza. The camera wasn't hurtling through space. The party wasn't dancing and carousing, and hard work isn't making money.

Maybe you're thinking, So what? I didn't think the phone was eating the pizza. I understood what the writer was saying.

Maybe so. But you do not want to invite you reader to say, "Huh? What's going on here?" And that's precisely what misplaced modifiers do—they cause the reader to pause, even if only for a milli-second, and during that pause, the idea surfaces that the writer, just maybe, has no idea what he or she is talking about. Not good.

Also, the sentences are short, clear examples of the misplaced modifiers. When your sentence gets long and complicated, the danger of misplaced modifiers grows and becomes more insidious, because when things get complicated, readers don't only pause, they also get genuinely confused. And then they will be disgusted with you, the writer. Again, not good.

---

### The Rule
Put modifying phrases next to their subjects.

---

# Embarrassing Moments In The Land Of Misplaced Modifiers

An ad for Natural Ultra Plus pads:

*So incredibly thin, you'll never know it's there!*

See the misplaced modifier? What follows the comma should be what is *so incredibly thin*—but the *pad* is incredibly thin, not *you*. But copywriters are anything but stupid. This may be a perfect example of an intentional misplaced modifier, giving the subtle impression that **you** *are incredibly thin*. The ad compliments as it advertises.

An ad for Pacific bathing suits:

*We can fit you in a swimsuit that fits and flatters—right over the phone!*

That must be some bathing suit, if you look good in it over the phone. They mean that they can fit you right over the phone, not that the suit flatters over the phone.

One more, an ad for a motorcycle company:

*While pleasing to your eye, the air passing over and around the body hardly notices it.*

We hope the visuals that went with this text were dazzling because let's face it, that sentence is hopeless. *The air* isn't *pleasing to your eye*, and while we're at it, what does the *it* stand for anyway? The body? The air? We give up.

---

## Quick Quiz #29

### Misplaced Modifiers

***Pick the best answer.***

1. <u>Although nearly completed</u>, the analysts stopped working on the report to have dinner.

   A) Although nearly completed
   B) Although they were nearly completed
   C) In spite of being nearly completed
   D) Although it was nearly completed
   E) Nearing completion

2. <u>Added to the raise and a company car</u>, Bob demanded a four-day work week.

   A) Added to the raise and a company car
   B) In addition to the raise and a company car
   C) In adding to the raise and a company car
   D) Not only a raise and a company car
   E) In addition to the raise and wanting a company car

3. Mowing the many-acred lawn, <u>the skies began to darken and Bob went inside.</u>

   A) the skies began to darken and Bob went inside
   B) the skies began to darken, so Bob went inside
   C) Bob went inside, being as the skies began to darken
   D) Bob, the skies darkening, went inside
   E) Bob saw the skies begin to darken and went inside.

Grammar Smart

4. <u>Depressed and sorrowfully inadequate</u>, the job seems to be too much for Bob.

   A) Depressed and sorrowfully inadequate
   B) Feeling depressed and sorrowfully inadequate
   C) Since he was depressed and sorrowfully inadequate
   D) Being that he was depressed and sorrowfully inadequate
   E) Being depressed and sorrowfully inadequate

5. After stocking up on potato chips, ice cream, videos, and cheap wine, <u>lying all day on the sofa seemed preferable to</u> showing up at the office.

   A) lying all day on the sofa seemed preferable to
   B) laying on the sofa all day seemed preferable to
   C) Bob preferred lying all day on the sofa to
   D) Bob was preferring lying on the sofa all day over
   E) lying all day on the sofa was preferable to

# D. Faulty Comparison

Examples from the Masters:

*Power in defense of freedom is greater than power in behalf of tyranny and oppression.*

−Malcolm X

*I doubt if the texture of Southern life is any more grotesque than that of the rest of the nation...*

−Flannery O'Connor

*The real problem is not whether machines think but whether men do.*

−B.F. Skinner

Let's do some analysis. Malcolm X is comparing two kinds of power: *power in defense of freedom,* and *power in behalf of tyranny. Power* is greater than *power;* equal parts are being compared.

Flannery O'Connor is comparing *texture* to *texture,* which is why she finishes her comparison by writing *than **that** of the rest of the nation.*

B. F. Skinner is not comparing men to machines—he is comparing the action, *think,* which is why he finished the comparison with the verb *do.*

Faulty comparison is a problem of clarity—either you leave the reader confused or you give an unintended meaning to your sentence. Remember:

---

## The Rule
Say what you mean.

---

Take a look at this example:

Pinky loves me more than Bob.

Could mean:

Pinky loves me more than Bob does.

**Or:** Pinky loves me more than she loves Bob.

A faulty comparison is not just a grammatical error, it could lead to romantic disaster. So:

---

## The Rule

When comparing actions, make sure to include both verbs, and the correct subject pronoun.

---

Bob hit more homers than Ralph *did*.

**Or:** Bob hit more homers than *did* Ralph.

**Not:** Bob hit more homers than Ralph.

Gomez works harder than I *do*.

**Or:** Gomez works harder than I. (the *do* is understood.)

**Not:** Gomez works harder than me.

Faulty comparisons also occur when comparing nouns.

Darlene's socks are uglier than Annabelle.

Note that this sentence could mean one of two things.

Darlene's socks are uglier than Annabelle is.

**Or:** Darlene's socks are uglier than Annabelle's socks.

Another quick path to confusion is seen in the following sentence:

Unlike her earlier work, which was characterized by thorough analysis and research, Roxanne seems to have become too bored with her subject to do an acceptable job.

This sentence fails to compare equal parts. *Unlike her earlier work* promises a comparison to some other work, but instead we get *Roxanne.* Fix it like this:

*Unlike her earlier work,* which was characterized by thorough analysis and research, *Roxanne's latest report* shows that she may have become too bored with her subject to do an acceptable job.

---

## The Rule
When comparing nouns, make sure both nouns are actually in the sentence, and that the nouns are comparable.

---

Pinky's allowance is more generous than *Billy's.*

**Or:** Pinky's allowance is more generous than Billy's *allowance.*

**Or:** Pinky's allowance is more generous than *that* of Billy.

**Not:** Pinky's allowance is more generous than Billy.

Her stocks and bonds were more valuable than *Bob's.*

**Or:** Her stocks and bonds were more valuable than *those* of Bob.

**Or:** Her stocks and bonds were more valuable than Bob's *stocks and bonds.*

**Not:** Her stocks and bonds were more valuable than Bob.

# Tips On Spotting Faulty Comparison

Remember that comparisons are almost always made with the words *than, as, like, unlike.* If you find yourself making faulty comparisons, look for these signal words in your sentences and make sure your comparisons read the way you mean them to.

---

## Quick Quiz #30
### Fixing Faulty Comparisons
*Correct the following sentences if necessary.*

1. Unlike mushrooms and other fungi, we cultivate tomatoes in as much sun as possible.

2. At the state fair, Pinky's tomatoes won more prizes than Bob.

3. Like asparagus, strawberries do not produce fruit in their first year.

4. Pinky had done more research on organic gardening than Bob.

---

# E. Idioms

If you've ever studied a foreign language, you know what idioms are—and how much trouble they can be. An idiom is simply, a peculiarity, a rule of usage that applies only to a particular instance. For example, to mean "We have got the same problem" we say "we're in the same boat," not "We're in the same car." Idioms include all of the expressions we use that are unique to English, including clichés: *eat crow, jump the gun, rain cats and dogs,* and so on. They also include preposition usage, which is what we're interested in here. If you are a native English-speaker, you probably, with a few exceptions, use idioms correctly without even thinking about it. If you're in doubt, you can try looking up the word in a dictionary, which often will list the appropriate preposition and usage.

# Idiom List #1

These idioms always take the same preposition–no matter what.

## With

**afflicted with:** I am *afflicted with* measles and dandruff.

**argue with:** Shut up and don't *argue with* me!

**comply with:** You must *comply with* the new regulations.

**consistent with:** Her speeches are not *consistent with* her actions.

**meet with (Things other than people. See Idiom List #3):** Are you certain that the new design *meets with* Federal regulations?

**tamper with:** The spy *tampered with* the engine and the plane when down.

## To

**according to:** *According* to Reagan, the 1980s were "Morning in America."

**analogous to:** The fallacy in her argument is that she makes everything *analogous to* everything else.

**averse to:** The man was *averse to* running for office.

**aversion to:** The woman had an *aversion to* politics.

**cater to:** He spent all day *catering to* his boss's whims.

**conform to:** The men refused to *conform to* the expectations of Mr. Dingdong.

**consider to be (the *to be* may be dropped):** He *considers* her *to be* the candidate best for the job.

Or: He *considers* her the candidate best for the job.

**equal to:** I am not *equal to* the task.

**forbid to:** I *forbid* you *to* sit on that chair.

**intend to (not *on doing*):** She *intends to* make partner before she is thirty.

**oblivious to:** He lives in a dream world, *oblivious to* reality.

**ought to:** She *ought to* put air in her tires.

**preferable to (not *than*):** Eating ice cream is *preferable to* cleaning the house.

**prior to:** *Prior to* the election, Democrats were subjected to background checks.

**superior to (not *than*):** Italian cooking is *superior to* English cooking.

**temerity to:** My boss had the *temerity to* ask me to pick up his dry cleaning.

**tie to:** In making her point, she *tied* her economic theory *to* sociological data.

**try to (not *and*):** *Try to* finish your work quickly so we can leave for the party.

## Of

**ask of:** What do you *ask of* life?

**capable of:** That cretin is *capable of* anything.

**composed of:** My wardrobe is *composed of* black pants and white shirts.

**desirous of:** I am *desirous of* more fun.

**in search of:** The girl was *in search of* a way to improve her backhand.

**necessity of/for:** Love is a *necessity of* a happy life.

**partake of:** After I eat the mousse I will *partake of* of the pudding.

# From

**buy from:** Don't *buy* anything *from* that sleazy operator.

**different from:** That potato is *different from* this one.

**divergent from:** I like the man even though his views are *divergent from* mine.

**prohibit from:** The parents do not *prohibit* their child *from* staying up late.

**separate from:** The man could not *separate* reality *from* fantasy.

# As

**define as:** Mental health has been *defined as* the ability to love and work.

**depict as:** Women are constantly *depicted as* ditzy victims in that action director's movies.

**regard as:** The public *regards* the 1980s *as* the "Greed Decade."

# For

**craving for:** I have a *craving for* chocolate bunnies.

**mistake for (not *as*):** Don't *mistake* me *for* a fool.

## On, Against, Over, At, In

**lavish on:** The man *lavished* presents *on* his child.

**prejudiced against:** I am *prejudiced against* beautiful people.

**dispute over:** The men had a *dispute over* money.

**chip at:** The sculptor *chipped* away *at* the marble in order to create a statue fit for a king.

**confide in:** Vicki Vale was overjoyed when Batman *confided in* her about his secret identity.

# Idiom List #2

These idioms take different prepositions, depending on the circumstance.

**agree to (a contract; implies concession or settlement):** I *agree to* your demands.

**agree with (a person, a place; implies harmony):** Paris *agrees with* me.

**angry about (an event, idea, etc.):** Bob is *angry about* the demonstration.

**angry at (a person):** Wanda is *angry at* me.

**angry with (a person; more confrontational than angry at):** Max is *angry with* me.

**compare to (to show similarity):** You can *compare* my copy *to* the original.

**compare with (to show difference and similarity):** His work can't *compare with* mine.

**consist in (to mean *reside* or *inhere*):** Success *consists in* valuing hard work.

**consist of (to mean *composed of*):** My meal *consists of* bread and jam.

**correspond to (to mean *match*; *be in agreement*):** The results of the experiment *correspond to* the predictions.

**correspond with (to mean *exchange letters*):** The lovers *corresponded with* each other while one of them was on location in Paris.

**decide on (a noun):** Let's *decide on* a place to eat.

**decide to (do something):** Let's *decide to* have some fun.

**differ with (to mean *disagree*):** I *differ with* him politically.

**differ from (to mean *unlike*):** Hats *differ from* shoes.

**different from (not *than*):** Hats are *different from* shoes.

**fail in (an attempt):** The man *failed in* his efforts.

**fail to (to something):** The man *failed to* finish his painting.

**practice for/to (when *practice* is a verb):** I have *practiced for* my recital. I am *practicing to* be an actor.

**practice of (when *practice* is a noun):** The *practice of* redlining is heinous.

**reconcile to (to mean *accept hardship*):** He was *reconciled to* his sad fate.

**reconcile with (a person):** After the fight, Pinky *reconciled with* Gomez.

**result from (when *result* is a verb):** A bad temper *results from* lack of sleep.

**result in (when *result* is a verb):** Lack of sleep *results in* bad temper.

**result of (when *result* is a noun):** A bad temper is *a result of* lack of sleep.

**sympathy for (to mean *have compassion for*):** I have *sympathy for* Bob.

**sympathy with (to mean *agreement; sharing of feelings*):** I have *sympathy with* your position.

# Idiom List #3

These words do not take prepositions. All of them are commonly misused.

**continue:** continue the meeting. Not: continue *with* the meeting.

**equally:** equally important. Not: equally *as* important.

**inside:** inside the box. Not: inside *of* the box.

**meet:** meet people. Not: meet *with* people. But you can meet *with* difficulties.

**name:** named Minister of Fun. Not: named *as* Minister of Fun.

**off:** I feel off my bed. Not: I fell off *of* my bed.

**tend:** tend the campfire. Not: tend *to* the campfire.

**visit:** visit your grandmother. Not: visit *with* your grandmother.

## Quick Quiz #31

### Idioms

*Fill in the blank with the correct preposition:*

1. His fashion sense is different (from, than) mine.

2. He is afflicted (by, with) color blindness.

3. He is prohibited (from buying, to buy) any clothes for me.

4. Compared (with, to) my clothes, his clothes are stunningly tasteless.

5. We often dispute (about, over) whether to wear sequins or leather.

# F. Diction

Diction is the correct choice of words. Once again, our second rule of writing:

---

## The Rule

Say what you mean.

---

When a writer makes a diction error, he shows himself to be either sloppy or ignorant. Not good. While it's true that if a word is misused often enough, its meaning may evolve so that the mistake becomes accepted usage, there are some words you need to be careful of. Here are some words that are often confused.

**advert:** *v* refer. In her thesis she *adverts* to Kierkegaard's theories.

**avert:** *v* to turn away. The sight was so horrible I *averted* my head.

**affect:** *v* to influence; to have an effect on. Overeating will *affect* his health. His policy will not *affect* economic recovery.

*n* behavior or mood, usually used in a psychological context. A cold, calm *affect*—even in the face of disaster—is often the hallmark of a sociopath.

**effect:** *v* cause to happen; bring about; result in. His election will *effect* changes in government policy. His policy will not *effect* economic recover.

*n* the result of an action. The effects of his decision will be felt for years.

When used as verbs, these two words have two distinct meanings: *affect* means *to influence* and *effect* means *cause to happen*. As verbs, you can grammatically use *affect/effect* in the same sentence, as above, but the meaning will be different. Use *affect* as a noun only when you are using it as a psychological term meaning *mood*.

**affection:** *n* fondness. She may not be in love, but she has *affection* for him.

**affectation:** *n* artificiality; a phony way of behaving. He picked up several *affectations* on his trip, including an English accent.

**alternate:** *v* succeeding by turns. She *alternated* eating string beans and oxtails.

**alternative:** *n* one of several possibilities. If you don't like what I made for dinner, suggest an *alternative*.

Avoid using *alternate* as a noun, unless you are talking about an *alternate* juror or an *alternate* delegate, in the sense of replacement or substitute. If you want to imply choice, use *alternative*.

**allusion:** *n* indirect reference. The new novel is full of *allusions* to Beckett and Sartre.

**illusion:** *n* something that misleads or gives a wrong impression. The young actress said that her job was to create the *illusion* that she was eighty years old and close to death.

**ambiguous:** *adj* uncertain; thought of in two different ways. His letter was *ambiguous*—I'm not sure if he is arriving tomorrow or next week.

**ambivalent:** *adj* contradictory; having opposite feeling about something at the same time. I am *ambivalent* about my new job; I love it and hate it.

*Ambivalent* does not mean *indifferent*. Keep in mind that *ambiguous* means *obscure*; *ambivalent* does not.

---

**can:** *v* to be able. I *can* leap tall building in a single bound.

**may:** *v* to be permitted. The professor said I *may* skip class if I get the notes from Bob. *May* I see your etchings?

**common:** *adj* shared. The two Democrats had a *common* purpose.

**mutual:** *adj* reciprocal. Necessary to any friendship is *mutual* respect.

---

To say: "We have a mutual friend" would be incorrect—better to say "we have a friend in common."

---

**compliment:** *n* expression of admiration. She *complimented* me on my shoes.

**complement:** *n* counterpart; helpful addition. The limes were a perfect *complement* to the beer.

**contemptible:** *adj* worthy of scorn. Her behavior is *contemptible.*

**contemptuous:** *adj* expressing scorn. I was *contemptuous* of her behavior.

---

This pair is like *incredible/incredulous*: one word (*contemptible*) describe the act, the other word (*contemptuous*) describes the way someone feels toward the act.

---

**continuous:** *adj* without interruption. The car alarm's *continuous* screeching lasted for three days.

**continual:** *adj* recurrent; stopping and starting. The *continual* bursts of lightning scared the dog.

**deduce:** *v* to figure out logically. The inspector *deduced* that the killer was near.

**deduct:** *v* to subtract. Please *deduct* the price of french fries from my bill.

**disinterested:** *adj* unbiased; objective. The man in charge of awarding prizes was *disinterested.*

**dispassionate:** *adj* unbiased; not swayed in judgment by feeling. As a *dispassionate* observer, I could say that the gymnast's performance was average.

**indifferent:** *adj* uncaring; not interested. She was *indifferent* to my invitation.

---

Don't mistake *disinterest* for lack of interest. *Uninterested* is sometimes used to mean *lack of interest,* but *indifferent* is better. *Dispassionate* does not mean *passionless* or *without erotic feeling.*

---

**emigrate:** *v* to move out of a country. My family *emigrated* from Poland.

**immigrate:** *v* to move into a country. My family *immigrated* to America.

---

It follows to say that my family *emigrated* from Poland and *immigrated* to America.

---

**eminent:** *adj* standing out; famous. The *eminent* philosopher has millions of followers.

**imminent:** *adj* happening soon. The election is *imminent.*

**immanent:** *adj* inherent; existing only within consciousness. Her *immanent* faith was revealed in all her actions.

**enormity:** *n* wickedness; hugeness. The *enormity* of Jeffrey Dahmer's acts became clear as details of his cannibalism were released. Or: Neighbors were dispirited by the *enormity* of the house being built next to theirs. (The second usage of *enormity*, to mean immensity, is a hot point of argument among those who argue about these things. The main point of this entry is to make sure you understand the first definition of *enormity*, to mean *a great and terrible crime*.)

**enormousness:** *n* hugeness. The *enormousness* of the job ahead made Bob want to get back in bed.

**felicitous:** *adj* appropriate. The casting of Michelle Pfeiffer as a beautiful woman is certainly *felicitous.*

**fortuitous:** *adj* happening by chance. What is more *fortuitous* than finding a winning lottery ticket lying in the gutter?

**fortunate:** *adj* lucky. I was *fortunate* enough to inherit some money.

---

The trouble with *fortuitous* and *felicitous* is that they are used interchangeably to mean lucky. *Fortuitous* is the luckier of the two; *felicitous* mean apt.

---

**former:** *n* in a list of two items, the first one.

**latter:** *n* in a list of two items, the second one.

---

I went to Paris and Rome; I bought clothes in the *former* and shoes in the *latter*. (That means clothes were bought in Paris and shoes were bought in Rome.)

---

**healthful:** *adj* conducive to health; giving health. The nutritionist recommended I stop eating potato chips and start a *healthful* diet.

**healthy:** *adj* in good health. I quit smoking in order to feel *healthy.*

Another way to look at this is that people, animals, and plants can be *healthy*; climates, diets, and exercise programs can be *healthful.*

---

**implicit:** *adj* implied or hinted at. There was a threat *implicit* in his request.

**explicit:** *adj* directly stated, not ambiguous. She was *explicit* when she said that if I miss the deadline I will fail the course.

**imply:** *v* to hint or express indirectly. Glaring at me, she *implied* that I was in big trouble.

**infer:** *v* to deduce. I *inferred* from her angry expression that I was in big trouble.

---

To keep this straight remember that the writer or speaker *implies*; the reader or listener *infers.*

---

**incredible:** *adj* unbelievable. His story of seeing an alien was *incredible.*

**incredulous:** *adj* unbelieving. I was *incredulous* when I heard his story about the alien.

---

*Incredulous* always applies to people—people are *incredulous* when they have a hard time believing something. An event is *incredible* when it is hard to believe.

---

**ingenious:** *adj* clever. He wrote an ingenious piece of software.

**ingenuous:** *adj* open; not crafty. We can hardly suspect her of conspiracy; her manner is so *ingenuous.*

**libel:** *n, v* written statement of defamation; to defame. After it printed a story claiming that she was drunk and disorderly, Carol Burnett sued *The National Enquirer* for *libel.*

**slander:** *n, v* spoken statement of defamation; to defame. When he gave a speech in which he distorted his opponent's record, the candidate exposed himself to charges of *slander.*

---

Both of these have the same effect: to make untrue statements in order to hurt someone's reputation. The difference is simply that *libel* is written and *slander* is spoken.

---

**militate:** *v* to have influence or weight. His shortness *militated* against his being drafted by the Knicks.

**mitigate:** *v* to soften; mollify. His soft voice *mitigated* the harshness of his words.

**nauseated:** *adj* feeling sick to one's stomach. The smell of rotten meat makes me *nauseated.*

**nauseous:** *adj* causing nausea. The smell of rotten meat is *nauseous.*

---

Use *nauseated* to describe how you feel; use *nauseous* to describe what is making you feel *nauseated.*

---

**practical:** *adj* useful; not theoretical. Wanda is anything but dreamy; she is the most *practical* person I know.

**practicable:** *adj* possible; feasible. The plan to revive the economy sounds good, but is it *practicable?*

---

Generally, people are *practical*, plans are *practical* or *practicable.*

---

**principal:** *adj* most important. His *principal* objective is to revive the economy.
*n* the person in charge of a public school, university, or college"
The *principal* ordered me to stay after school.

**principle:** *n* a doctrine; a moral. His actions show he has high *principles*.

---

What people do wrong is to try to use *principle* as an adjective: My *principle* goal is to make a heap of money, is incorrect. It should be: My *principal* goal is to make a heap of money. *Principal* as a noun is the person you had to talk to if you got in trouble at school.

---

**respectfully:** *adv* showing respect. The girl behaved *respectfully* toward her grandmother.

**respectively:** *adv* in the given order. Bob and Harry were an accountant and a lawyer, *respectively*.

**sensory:** *adj* relating to sensation. Swimming in cold water and lying on hot sand are different *sensory* experiences.

**sensuous:** *adj* relating to the senses. He is a *sensuous* writer. Listening to opera is a *sensuous* experience.

**sensual:** *adj* relating to the gratification of the senses; lewd. She was so consumed with *sensual* pleasures she could hardly get her work done.

---

Use *sensory* to mean *clinical sensation*. Use *sensual* to mean *sexual and excessive*. Use *sensuous* to mean *sensitive to sensation in the broadest way*, not particularly the sexual way—you could be a *sensuous* writer and a monk.

---

**tortuous:** *adj* winding; twisting. The road to the castle was *tortuous*.

**torturous:** *adj* excruciatingly painful. The deep sea diver had a *torturous* ascent to the surface.

It's easy to mix up these two, because of the similarity in spelling, and in fact, they derive from the same root, *tortus*, which is Latin for *twist*. But currently the second word, *torturous*, relates specifically to torture and not necessarily twisting.

# Things Never To Say, Words Never To Use

Certain diction problems aren't a matter of confusing two words, but a matter of out-and-out non-English. Often these problems come up when someone is trying to sound fancy and official. In language, as in life, simpler is better.

**irregardless:** no such word. Use *regardless*.

**being that, being as:** vulgar and pretentious. Use *because*. Not: Being that I am the only one with a driver's license, I think I should drive. Instead say: Because I am the only one with a driver's license, I think I should drive.

**where at:** Forget the *at*! Where is the party? Not: Where is the party *at*?

**as to:** also pretentious. We wondered *about* his health. Not: We wondered *as to* his health.

**could of, would of:** Say *could have, would have.* This problem may have gotten started by the similar sound of *could've* and *would've*—but on paper, the *of* in place of the verb is ridiculous.

**had ought:** *had* and *ought* don't quite mean the same thing. She *had* to go. She *ought* to go. Not: She *had ought* to go.

**in regards to:** Use *regarding* or *in regard to*.

**double negatives:** She didn't come. Not: She *didn't never* come. He wanted none. Not: He *didn't* want *none*.

**owing to the fact that:** wordy. Use *because*.

**in the event that:** wordy. Use *if*.

# Words We Find Irritating

There are certainly better choices than the following. These words aren't wrong per se, but they will give your writing a tired and bureaucratic quality.

| | |
|---|---|
| maximize | utilize |
| finalize | prioritize |
| impact (as a verb) | value-added |
| probabilistic | basically |
| doable | facilitate |

## Quick Quiz #32

### Diction

*Correct the diction in the following passage:*

Jasper's family emigrated to Brazil because they found the superficiality of American culture to be truly incredulous. Jasper's father was an immanent plastic surgeon, so one could say that his very career was marked by attention to superficiality, since he only performed cosmetic surgery.

The principle reason they moved to Brazil was that the beaches were terrific. The sea had a calming affect on Jasper, who unfortunately did not usually behave respectively towards his parents, and whose life was characterized by an obsession for sensory experience. Jasper's family could have moved away from their former home, but they were disinterested in any other country but Brazil, and considered no other alternates.

# G. Redundancy

Redundancy is repeatedly saying the same thing twice, over again, more than once. A redundancy mistake causes the problem we've mentioned before—it makes your writing seem overblown and not thought out, leaving your reader to wonder whether you are asleep at the wheel. Below are some common redundancies.

small in size

circulate around

true fact

joint partnership

close to the point of

reason...is because

reason why...is because

in this day and time

consensus of opinion

pair of twins (unless you mean four people)

cooperate together, collaborate together

close proximity

contemporary writer of today

if and when

mingle together

new innovation

joint cooperation

3:00 A.M. in the morning

6:00 P.M. at night

# H. Voice And Mood

And finally, we have a few last words on verbs.

## Voice

If you have a choice, use the active voice, in which the subject acts, instead of passive voice, in which something is done to your subject.

**Active voice:** Wanda *cooked* collard greens.

**Passive voice:** The collard greens *were cooked by* Wanda.

Active voice has a verb that takes a direct object. In passive voice, the object is turned into the subject, and the verb is a form of the verb *to be* plus a past participle. Active voice is the stronger form of expression.

## Mood

Yes, even verbs can have moods—three of them, in fact. Only the subjunctive causes any problems.

**Indicative mood:** for statement of fact or asking a question.

> He's back.
>
> His teeth are green.
>
> Are you eating cheese?

**Imperative mood:** for commands or directions.

> Do it now.
>
> Call me.
>
> Follow the road to the foundry.

**Subjunctive mood:** for statements that are contrary to fact, or for *that* clauses of order, demand, or recommendation.

1. *Contrary to fact* simply mean *not true.* For example:

> The girl said that if she were a boy, she would want to play for the Knicks.

A girl is speaking, so the clause *if she were a boy* is a statement contrary to fact, which means we use the subjunctive.

2. *That* clauses of order, demand, recommendations. For example:

> The girl demanded that she be allowed to try out for the Knicks.

Here's what is different about the subjunctive mood. *She* is usually conjugated with *was. She was,* not *she were.* And in the second example, the regular conjugation would be *she is allowed,* not *she be allowed.*

But the subjunctive conjugation is different. The subjunctive for the verb *to be* is *be* for present tense (she *be* allowed) and *were* for past tense.

The subjunctive for all other verbs is third person plural—the verb that goes with *they.*

The best way to understand the subjunctive is to look at some examples.

> If it *were* August, I would go to the beach.

> She ordered that the door *be* closed.

> He recommends that she *write* her paper tonight.

> If I *were* you, I would go back to bed.

# I. Gender-Neutral Writing

The term *gender-neutral writing* refers to writing that avoids making unjustified assumptions about the gender of the person it describes. For example, writers have traditionally used the pronoun *he* to refer to an anonymous or generic person ("if a writer wants to be successful, *he* needs to understand grammar"). But times have changed. These days, the readers of your work, as well as the people you are writing about, are likely to be of both genders equally. It's in your best interest to make your reader feel included by your choice of words, so you should strive for gender-neutral writing at all times.

This doesn't mean that you have to butcher your writing. At most it will mean a little extra work, but in return you will reduce the risk of alienating your readers with language that could be interpreted as chauvinistic or outmoded. And the extra time you put into crafting your sentences carefully will probably make your writing more precise and easier to read. Finally, you should use gender-neutral language because it follows our golden rule: avoid trouble. If a sentence could be misinterpreted, find another way to write it. The following is a quick guide to writing in a gender-neutral fashion.

## The Obvious Stuff: Nouns

Whenever possible, avoid using generic terms based on the word "man."

| Not preferred | Preferred |
|---|---|
| Man | human, personality |
| Mankind | humanity, people, human beings |
| Man-made | manufactured, synthetic, artificial |
| Man-hours | work-hours, staff-hours |

All I need to complete this job are a few good people.

Not: All I need to complete this job are a few good men.

Also, use the neutral form of job titles.

| Not preferred | Preferred |
|---|---|
| mailman | letter carrier |
| congressman | representative |
| policeman | police officer |
| fireman | firefighter |
| steward/stewardess | flight attendant |
| chairman | chairperson, coordinator |

To protest this law, write to your congressional representative.

Not: To protest this law, write to your congressman.

# The Harder Stuff: Pronouns And Possessives

The trickier part of gender-neutral writing is learning how to deal with pronouns. Here are some ways you can write your sentences to avoid these pitfalls.

1. Use the plural *they* or *them.*

Because there is no gender-neutral singular pronoun in English, use the plural pronouns *they* and *them* to refer to people in general. The solution is to put everything in plural form.

*Students* should solve *their* own *problems.*

**Not:** Every student should solve *his* own problem.

2. Replace the possessive with *a, an,* or *the*.

Often there's no reason to use *his*—you can simply replace it with *a* or *the*.

Give each candidate *the* exam upon arrival.

**Not:** Give each candidate *his* exam as soon as he arrives.

3. Eliminate the pronoun or possessive.

In some cases, you can simply remove the pronoun or possessive, and the sentence will still be perfectly readable:

Anyone who wants an ice cream should bring three dollars
to class on Monday.

**Not:** Anyone who wants an ice cream should bring *his* three dollars
to class on Monday.

4. Replace *he* and *him* with *he or she* and *his* with *his or her*.

Each student should consult *his or her* advisor before registering.

**Not:** Each student should consult *his* advisor before registering.

Another way to fix this sentence would be to follow #2 above:

Each student should consult *an* advisor before registering.

5. Replace *he/him* with *you/your* or *one/one's* or another neutral noun.

If *you* want to prevent confusion, *you* should avoid using "he"
except when referring to a male.

**Not:** If a writer wants to prevent confusion, *he* should avoid
using the word "he", unless *he* is referring to a male.

If *one* wants to prevent confusion, *one* should avoid using the word "he" except when referring to a male. Also to prevent confusion, *writers* should avoid using the word "he" except when referring to a male.

# Summary

- **subject-verb agreement:** Subjects and verb must agree. Singular subjects take singular verbs, and plural subjects take plural verbs.

- **pronoun agreement:** Pronouns must agree with their antecedents. Singular pronouns stand in for singular nouns, and plural pronouns stand in for plural nouns.

- **parallel construction:** When making a list, put words, phrases, or clauses in the same form. Be consistent.

- **faulty comparison:** Compare apples to apples and oranges to oranges; that is, nouns to nouns and verbs to verbs. Don't leave part of the comparison out.

- **misplaced modifier:** Modifiers, whether single words or phrases, should be placed as close as possible to what is being modified. Look out for a participial phrase beginning the sentence.

- **idiom:** Use the right preposition with the right idiom. Unfortunately, idioms, by definition, have no standardized set of rules; you must learn them separately.

- **diction:** Use words correctly. Be careful not to confuse the meanings of similar-looking words.

- **redundancy:** Do not say the same thing twice, needlessly. Be concise. Be clear.

- **voice:** The two voices are active, in which the subject acts, and passive, in which something is done to the subject. Use active voice if possible.

- **mood:** Verbs, or sentences, have three moods: indicative mood makes a statement or asks a question; imperative mood gives a direction or makes a command; subjunctive mood is used for statements contrary to fact, or in *that* clauses of order, demand or recommendation. Subjunctive is the only mood that puts anyone in a bad mood.

# Batting Practice, Part 3

These drills cover errors from Part 3: parallel construction, misplaced modifiers, faulty comparison, idiom, diction, redundancy, voice, and mood.

## Drill 1

*Pick the best answer.*

1. The stress that comes from repressing one's true desire <u>is as great or greater than is brought about by insufficient rest, overwork, and poor diet</u>.

    A) is as great or greater than is brought about by insufficient rest, overwork, and poor diet

    B) that is as great or greater than that brought about by insufficient resting, overworking and poor diet

    C) is as great as or greater than that of insufficient rest, overwork, and poor diet

    D) is at least as great as that brought about by insufficient rest, overwork, and poor diet

    E) is at least as great as the stress brought about through resting insufficiently, overwork, and poor diet

2. In New England <u>dairy farmers belong to collectives, where their milk, cheese, and other products are pooled with the products of other farms, and which provides the farmers</u> with some security by stabilizing prices.

A) dairy farmers belong to collectives, where their milk, cheese, and other products are pooled with the products of other farms, and which provides the farmers

B) dairy farmers belong to collectives, in which their milk, cheese, and other products are pooled with the products of other farms, and which provide the farmers

C) a dairy farmer belongs to collectives, in which their milk, cheese, and other products are pooled with the products of other farms, and which provide the farmer

D) of the dairy farmers belong to a collective, in which their milk, cheese, and other products are pooled with the products of other farms, providing the farmer

E) of the dairy farmers do belong to collectives, where their milk, cheese, and other products are being pooled with the products of other farms, which provides the farmers

3. Some dogs, unlike those kept strictly for pets, have serious work expected of them, <u>such as herding flocks of sheep, to warn their owners</u> when calves get separated from the herd, and acting as guards.

A) such as herding flocks of sheep, to warn their owners

B) such as herding flocks of sheep, warning their owners

C) like herding flocks of sheep, warning its owners

D) like being a herder for sheep, and warning their owners

E) like herding flocks of sheep and to warn its owners

4. Unlike buying individual stocks, which requires doing business with a stockbroker, an investor in a private company can do business directly with the executives of the company itself.

A) an investor in a private company can do business directly

B) an investor, doing business with a private company, can deal directly

C) investing in a private company allows the investor to do business directly

D) an investment in a private company allows the investor to do business directly

E) an investment in a company that is private allows the investor to do direct business

5. If the president was a woman, the country might see a real dedication to family values, marked with policy changes such as the passage of a bill mandating time off for children, and attention to education that goes beyond lip service.

A) If the president was a woman, the country might see a real dedication to family values, marked with policy changes such as the passage of a bill mandating time off for childbirth, and attention to education that goes beyond lip service

B) If the president was a woman, the country might see a real dedication to family values, marked by policy changes such as the passage of a bill mandating time off for childbirth, and attention to education that goes beyond lip service

C) If the president was a woman, the country might see a real dedication to family values, marked with policy changes like the passage of a bill that mandates time off for childbirth, and attention to education that goes beyond lip service

D) Were the president a woman, the country might see a real dedication to family values, marked by policy changes like passing a bill that would mandate time off for childbirth, and paying attention to education beyond lip service

E) If the president were a woman, the country might see a real dedication to family values, marked by policy changes such as the passage of a bill mandating time off for childbirth, and attention to education that goes beyond lip service

# Drill 2

*Find the error. If there is no error, pick choice E.*

1. Although many workplaces have become more flexible, in the
       A                  B

   1990s women still must choose between having a serious career
                     C

   or having a family. _____
     D          E

2. In this day and time, sexual harassment is dealt with publicly,
         A                              B

   and is often covered by the media, whereas before the Anita Hill-
                                 C

   Clarence Thomas debacle, it was usually handled privately, or
                            D

   not at all. _____
       E

3. The reporter, stopping us on the street, asked Bob and I whether we
             A                B      C

   believed the testimony of Clarence Thomas or that of Anita Hill. _____
                             D          E

4. Speaking before the Senate committee, Anita Hill's demeanor
                               A

   was reserved and solemn; Clarence Thomas, on the other hand,
                                 B

   demonstrated tremendous force and self-righteous rage. _____
     C                    D      E

5. Partly because it was televised, the Anita Hill–Clarence Thomas
         A

   hearings inflamed the nation, forced everyone to take sides, and
                             B

   was causing sexual harassment to be debated in living rooms and
     C                    D

   workplaces across the country. _____
                E

# Drill 3

*Correct the following passage.*

Being as he kept breaking out in hives, Boris decided on going to a doctor, although since he had not been to a doctor in years, he had to look up *Doctors* in the Yellow Pages. On the way to Dr. Wrigley's office, Boris drove slowly, looking intently at the road ahead, playing his radio at ear-shattering volume, and he scratched his ever-growing hives.

Dr. Wrigley took one look at him and began prescribing ointments and salves that would take care of the itching. Inspecting a particularly large and glowing hive on Boris's rear end, his response was to laugh heartily.

"Boris, my dear man," the doctor said, "you may not believe me, but when one breaks out in hives as stunning as these, one must take steps to relieve the stress in your life."

"What stress?" asked Boris. "I have a job that is totally undemanding and I never get into disagreements with anyone."

"You are one of those men who is leading a desperate life of non-engagement," said Dr. Wrigley. "If I was you I'd read Sartre. And stop scratching."

Boris got huffy. He shouted that he loved his life more than the doctor, and fled the office without remembering to pick up the proscriptions. The affect of Boris's visit to the doctor was to unleash the animal in him, which had the surprising affect of curing his hives.

# PART 4

# Punctuation

# To Semicolon Or Not To Semicolon

It's time to deal with those tiny scratch-marks known as punctuation. Like syntax, punctuation can be part of a writer's style; in some instances, the rules are fuzzy enough that a writer can choose his or her manner of punctuating to suit his or her purpose. Hemingway, to go back to our example in the introduction, was a big fan of the period. Simple sentence, period. Henry James needed dozen of semicolons and thousands of commas, parentheses, and dashes just to get through one sentence.

The purpose of punctuation is to make the act of reading your sentences easier and to make the movement of the eye across the page smoother. The purpose of punctuation is not to draw attention to itself—you want the reader to pay attention to what you have written, not to the placement of commas. Try to cultivate a natural, easygoing punctuation style. If you happen to read something in which the punctuation seems irritating, take a minute to figure out what, precisely, seems bothersome about it.

This chapter is not meant to be complete; it covers basic rules, common confusions, and common errors.

# A. The Period

The period signals a full stop.

## Rules For Periods

1. Put a period at the end of a sentence.

2. Put a period after most abbreviations: Mr. Wifflamoo, Mrs. Dingdong, Pres. Clinton, Nov. 12, A.M., etc. Some abbreviations don't need periods: FBI, NBC, JFK (government organizations, networks, monograms).

3. (Put a period at the end of a complete sentence enclosed by parentheses.) Put a period outside parentheses if what is enclosed by parentheses is not a complete sentence (like this).

4. Put a period inside quotation marks: The sign said "No Admittance."

# B. The Question Mark

A question mark signals that the preceding statement is a question.

## Rules For Question Marks

1. Use a question mark at the end of a question sentence.

> Wherefore art thou, Romeo?

> Is it love?

2. If the question is a quotation, put quotation marks after the question mark.

> He asked, "May I have this dance?"

> "How do I look?" she asked.

3. If the question is not part of the quotation, put the question mark after the quotation marks.

> What do you think of "No new taxes"?

> Do you believe in "an eye for an eye"?

# C. The Exclamation Point

Exclamation points are used for emphasis! Excitement! Surprise!

## Rules For Exclamation Points

1. Use an exclamation point after an exclamation.

Get lost!

Aha!

We won!

2. Don't get carried away with exclamation points. The only error generally committed is using an exclamation point to try to give writing more emphasis than it deserves. And never use more than one!

# D. The Comma

The comma is the most abused punctuation mark, possibly because writers are sometimes so worried about following rules that they forget to pay attention to the way the words sound when spoken. Commas help a reader understand the rhythm of the sentence. If you are having comma problems, try saying your sentence out loud and listening for natural pauses. The function of a comma is to slow the reader down briefly—to make the reader pause. The omission of a comma can allow phrases and clauses to crash into one another, thereby confusing the reader.

Commas can influence the meaning of your sentence. Consider the following:

> Although I wanted to kill Max, I controlled myself.

> Although I wanted to kill, Max, I controlled myself.

In the first sentence Max is the person I wanted to kill; in the second sentence I am talking to Max about my desire to kill something else. The comma controls the meaning.

Let's look at another:

> The food tastes terrible, however the cook fixes it.

> The food tastes terrible; however, the cook fixes it.

In the first sentence, the food tastes terrible no matter how the cook fixes it. In the second sentence, the cook improves the taste of the food. Again, the comma controls the meaning.

# Rules For Commas

1. Use a comma to separate two independent clauses connected by the following: *and, but, or, nor, for.*

    Bob was usually a quiet man, *but* he screamed upon entering the room.

    The strange man lying under the table appeared to be dead, *or* just possibly he was only napping.

    If the independent clauses are short, you may omit the comma.

    The man was still and his foot was bleeding.

    His hat was on but his pants were off.

2. Use a comma to separate elements in a list or series; the comma is a substitute for *and.* Some people omit the final comma, but we prefer to leave it in.

    Bob tried to breathe, to keep from fainting, and to remember his first aid.

    Next to the man was a bassoon, a water balloon, and a raccoon.

3. Use a comma to separate introductory phrases and clauses from the independent clause.

> After catching his breath, Bob squatted next to the man and took his pulse.

> When he felt nothing, Bob picked up the bassoon and blew.

> Although he had never played a bassoon before, he somehow managed to make beautiful music.

If the introductory phrase is short, you may omit the comma.

> After dark they stopped playing basketball.

But be careful. Always use a comma if omitting it could cause confusion.

> When Bob began to eat, rats ran across the carpet.

> **Not:** When Bob began to eat rats ran across the carpet.

> Before leaving, Bob heard the man sneeze.

> **Not:** Before leaving Bob heard the man sneeze.

4. In a series of adjectives, use a comma if the adjectives could also be separated by *and*.

>The nimble, fat raccoon began to poke at the water balloon.

>(Could write as: The nimble and fat raccoon...)

If the *and* doesn't fit, leave out the comma:

>The man's white cotton shirt was balled up in a corner.

>(Wouldn't write as: The man's white and cotton shirt...)

If this rule seems confusing, try reading the sentence aloud. If you make a slight pause between adjectives, put in commas. Otherwise, leave them out. Another test: if you can change the order of the adjectives, put in commas. For example:

>The handsome, brilliant scholar

>**Or:** The brilliant, handsome scholar

>The frilly party dress

>**Not:** The party frilly dress

5. Use commas to set off clauses, but don't use commas for defining clauses. (Quick review: a defining, or restrictive, clause is one that can't be left out of a sentence. Clauses that don't define can be lifted from the sentence without changing the meaning. Also, a defining clause specifies which part of a larger group we are talking about.)

Bananas that are green taste tart. (*that are green* defines which bananas we mean)

Bananas, which grow in the tropics, do not need refrigeration. (*which grow in the tropics* refers to all bananas. The clause can be lifted from the sentence without changing the meaning.)

Let's look at a sentence you could punctuate either way, depending on the meaning.

The men who were tired and hungry began eating sardines. (*who were tired and hungry* is a defining clause, telling us which men we mean)

The men, who were tired and hungry, began eating sardines. (*who were tired and hungry* describes all of the men, and doesn't differentiate these men from other men who weren't tired and hungry)

6. Words or phrases that interrupt the sentence should be set off by commas.

Now then, let's get down to work.

"Help me," he said, before falling down the stairs.

What the candidate promised, in fact, is
impossible to achieve.

Hello, I must be going.

7. Use commas to set off an appositive. An appositive is a word or phrase that explains or introduces the noun that precedes it.

Mrs. Bowden, my favorite teacher, is wearing a hat.

Ralphie, the president of the student council,
is on probation.

Remember that commas are one way to make your writing clear. Reading your sentences aloud is a very good way to find the natural place for commas, as is inspecting your sentences for ambiguity or confusion.

# E. The Semicolon

For some reason the semicolon is the most feared punctuation mark; it seems to inspire loss of confidence even in accomplished writers. The rules for semicolons are simple.

## Rules For Semicolons

1. Use a semicolon to link two independent clauses.

> To give a good party, you must consider the lighting; no one feels comfortable under the bright glare of fluorescent lights.

Note that the two clauses are connected in thought. Also—and this is the thing to understand about semicolons—you could use a comma and a conjunction in place of the semicolon.

> To give a good party, you must consider the lighting, *since* no one feels comfortable under the bright glare of fluorescent lights.

2. Use a semicolon to separate elements in a list if the elements are long or if the elements themselves have commas in them.

> To get completely ready for your party, you should clean your house; make sure your old, decrepit stereo works; prepare a lot of delicious, strange food; and expect odd, antisocial, and frivolous behavior on the part of your guests.

3. Semicolons belong outside quotation marks.

> One man at the party sat in a corner and read "The Adventures of Bob"; he may have been shy, or he may have found "The Adventures of Bob" too exciting to put down.

# F. The Colon

A colon tells a reader to pay attention to what follows.

## Rules For Colons

1. Use a colon when making a list.

> There are four ingredients necessary to a good party: music, lighting, food, and personality.

2. A colon is sometimes used to introduce a quotation or an explanation.

> On Saturday President Bush made the following statement: "This country's economy is in trouble!"

3. A colon must follow an independent clause. The information after the colon may be an independent clause or a dependent clause.

# G. Parentheses

## Rules For Parentheses

1. Use parentheses to enclose extra material (explanations, asides, etc.) that would otherwise interrupt the flow of the sentence.

   If you go skin diving at night (an adventure for only the most experienced divers) you can observe strange and amazing phenomena.

   As she whipped the cream (after making sure the ingredients were very cold) she told us she had made mousse only once before.

2. Put a period inside the parentheses if what is inside the parentheses is a complete sentence. (See Rules for Periods, on pages 147-48.)

3. Don't put a comma after the parentheses unless the sentence would require it anyway.

# H. The Dash

Dashes can be used in place of a colon or parentheses. Some people feel that dashes greater emphasis. Whether you use dashes is your choice—they are optional.

## Rules For Dashes

1. Use one dash in place of a colon, following the rules for colons.

We finished our tasks in record time—one hour!

**Or:** We finished our tasks in record time: one hour!

**2.** You can use dashes instead of parentheses.

If you come to my house—take a left after crossing the bridge—please bring some turnips and an oboe.

**Or:** If you come to my house (take a left after crossing the bridge) please bring some turnips and an oboe.

# I. The Apostrophe

The apostrophe is used to show ownership. Most of the time, it presents no confusion: Bob's bassoon, the woman's finger. The tricky part is using an apostrophe when the owner is plural.

## Rules For Apostrophes

1. If the plural noun doesn't end in -s, add an apostrophe and -s. (This is the easy part.)

the women's fingers

the bacteria's growth

the cat's hairballs

2. If the plural ends in -s, just add an apostrophe.

the babies' bottoms

the horses' hooves

the politicians' promises

3. If the word is a proper noun that ends in -s, add an apostrophe and an -s. (This is the part people get wrong.)

Yeats's poem

Ross's riddle

Chris's crisis

4. One exception is the possessive of the pronoun *it*, which is *its* (no apostrophe). The word *it's* (with apostrophe) is the contraction for *it is*, and not the possessive.

> We're giving the robot *its* weekly check-up today.

> **Not:** We're giving the robot *it's* weekly check-up today.

> *It's* a beautiful day in the neighborhood.

> **Not:** *Its* a beautiful day in the neighborhood.

If this strikes you as confusing, notice that the word *it* is treated similarly to the words *he*, *she*, and *they*. When apostrophes are added to these words, they become contractions: he's going to the store, she's going to bed, and they're going to work. The possessive pronouns do not contain apostrophes: his book, her food, their table, its mountains.

# J. The Hyphen

A hyphen separates compound words. In etymological evolution, two words may be separate, then joined by a hyphen, then joined altogether. For instance, *week end* changed to *week-end* and then to *weekend*. The best way to find out about a particular word is to look it up in the dictionary.

## Rules For Hyphens

1. If the pair of words forms an adjective that comes before the noun, use a hyphen.

   well-known felon

   first-class work

2. If the adjective pair comes after the noun, you don't need a hyphen.

   His crimes are well known.

   His work is always first class.

3. Use a hyphen for fractions acting as adjectives:

   He drank one and two-thirds cans of beer.

But not for fractions acting as nouns:

   Two thirds of the people have gone home.

4. Use a hyphen to differentiate certain words:

   He recollected his adventure in Guam.

   He re-collected the money.

   She recovered from the flu.

   She re-covered the sofa.

# K. Quotation Marks

The main problem with quotation marks is knowing whether other punctuation marks belong inside or outside of them. For periods, commas, and question marks, look back in this section to A, B, and C, respectively.

## Rules For Quotation Marks

1. Put quotation marks around direct quotations.

   "Here's Johnny!" said Nicholson.

2. If you have a quote within a quote, put single quotation marks around it.

   "He said, 'I can't live without you.'"

   "Stop!" said Victor, "or I'll yodel 'My Wild Irish Rose.'"

3. The use of quotation marks to show irony has become tired; avoid it if you can.

### Billy Wifflamoo, the Final Chapter

*Punctuate the following passage.*

Billy had several more visits from the aliens sometimes they ate snacks on his Buick sometimes they played music and danced One alien in particular became Billy's friend The alien taught Billy some good tricks a foolproof method for shooting foul shots a lip smacking recipe for tadpoles and a way to make his eyes change color at will.

Later in life Billy found himself married with two small children living in a peaceful suburb He said that he couldn't be happier

You miss the aliens said his wife one night putting the children to bed

She was right His Buick had long ago gone to the scrap heap and the aliens once his friends did not appear anymore Sometimes it made Billy sad but he threw himself into his work as an accountant for a chain of dry cleaners and occasionally he made a little money making bets on his foul-shooting Although he lived a sedate quiet life he always treasured the days of snacking with the aliens.

# PART 5

# Commonly-Asked Questions And Answers

**Q:** Is it okay to being a sentence with *because?*

**A:** Sure, why not? For some reason "Don't start a sentence with because" is the one rule people remember from grammar classes, but there is no such rule. What you can't do is offer up a subordinate clause that begins with *because* and try to pass it off as a complete sentence. *Because it was raining* is not a complete sentence; it's a subordinate clause that needs to be attached to an independent clause. *Because it was raining, I took my umbrella* is fine. For more on sentence fragments, see Part 2.

**Q:** What about beginning a sentence with *and?*

**A:** Technically, you'll be writing a fragment. But if you want to do it on purpose, for emphasis, go right ahead. Sentences beginning with *and* are the stock in trade of copywriters, so we're all used to seeing them; the important thing is not to use them without good reason. And that's that.

**Q:** Is it okay to end a sentence with a preposition?

**A:** This is another one of those rules that people get overexcited about. (See?) Strict adherence to this rule can make for some mighty awkward and pompous-sounding sentences. So yes, if you are writing formally, recast the sentence so that a preposition does not fall at the end—but don't bother if doing so makes your sentence sound unnaturally stiff. (Winston Churchill: "This is the sort of English up with which I will not put.")

**Q:** Is it okay to say "OK"?

**A:** In formal writing, no. In informal speech or writing, sure, it's OK—and you can spell it OK, O.K., or okay.

**Q:** **Is there a difference between *toward* and *towards*?**

**A:** *Towards* is British; *toward* is American. Choose accordingly.

**Q:** **I'm totally confused by *like* and *as*. Rescue me. Which do I use when?**

**A:** Fasten your seat belt. Even accomplished writers get lost on *like* and *as*, partly because the use of *like* in speech has gone completely out of control. *Like* is a preposition, not a conjunction. Use *like* to make a comparison: *He looks like me. She acts like the president. Like Bob, Pinky wears red socks.* In all three sentences we are making comparisons: *he* to *me*, *she* to *president*, *Bob* to *Pinky*. *Like* should be followed only by a noun or a noun phrase.

It would be false, and pompous, to say: *He looks as I* (do). *As does Bob, Pinky wears red socks.* (Don't be afraid to use *like*.) *She acts as a president* could be correct, if you mean that she is acting in the capacity of a president, that she is actually doing whatever presidents do. But if you only mean to compare her to a president, stay with *like*. *Like* never functions as a conjunction, so if your comparison involves action, use *as* or *as if*: *Winston tastes good, as a cigarette should. Ralph ran as if his life depended on it.* In both cases, the *as* or *as if* is a conjunction that joins two clauses.

We're not done yet. Another trouble spot is the confusion between *like* and *such as*. Remember that *like* is for comparisons. *Such as* means *for example: For breakfast he cooked local specialties such as grits and red-eye gravy.* To say *like grits and red-eye gravy* would be to say that he didn't actually cook grits and red-eye gravy but some other food that was similar to grits and red-eye gravy. See the difference?

**Q: What is a split infinitive?**

**A:** Remember that an infinitive is the form of the verb that begins with *to*. *To play, to speak, to flee.* If you insert a word between the *to* and the rest of the infinitive, you are guilty of splitting the infinitive to *happily* play, to *harshly* speak, to *quickly* flee. This is not a good idea, although it has become rampant even in good writing. If it doesn't lead to awkwardness and confusion, place your adverb on either side of the infinitive *to play* happily; *to speak* harshly; *to flee* quickly.

**Q: When should say *good*, and when should I say *well*?**

**A:** Good question. Strictly speaking, *good* is an adjective and *well* is an adverb, although *well* can also be used as an adjective in certain circumstances, such as in describing health, satisfaction, or appearance (with the verbs *appear, be, become, remain, seem, feel, smell, look, sound, taste*).

I did *well* on my test. (adverb)

I did *well*. (adjective, describing health)

The doughnuts were *good*. (good is always an adjective)

**Q: What about *bad* and *badly*?**

**A:** *Bad* is an adjective, and *badly* is an adverb. Say *I felt bad when I woke up.* Not: *I felt badly when I woke up.* Follow the rules for *good* and *well*.

**Q: Do you say *none is* or *none are*?**

**A:** It depends. *None* is an indefinite pronoun, usually treated as plural, unless you want to emphasize the individual parts, as in *not one single thing* or *no one single person*. When in doubt, go with the plural.

**Q:** **Please explain that ugly *who/whom* thing.**

**A:** Easy question. *Who* is the subject of a verb. *Whom* is never the subject of a verb. If you are confused, try to see whether you would use *she* or *her*. If *she* fits, use *who*. If *her* fits, use *whom*. *Who* is a subject pronoun; *whom* is an object pronoun.

*The girl asked who had called.* (*she* had called or *her* had called? *She* had called, so use *who*. *Who* is the subject of *had called*.)

*The girl asked whom she should call.* (should call *she* or should call *her*? Should call *her*, so use *whom*. *Whom* is the object of *should call*.)

In speech you can get away with using *who* for questions: *Whom did you call?* is correct, but no one is going to murder you for asking *Who did you call?* In writing, however, use *whom* when it's appropriate.

**Q:** **Is there a rule about *shall* and *will*?**

**A:** You bet. Use *shall* when there is implied intention: I *shall* return! Not: It *shall* be warm at the beach. You can also use *shall* for asking questions in the first person (*I* or *we*): *Shall* we dance? *Shall* I call you? Using *shall* in the second or third person implies a command or threat: You *shall* stay here until I say otherwise.

**Q: Is there a rule about using *due to*?**

**A:** Don't use it as a substitute for *because of*, or as a prepositional phrase. An effect is *due to* a cause.

> **Correct:** His tardiness was *due to* traffic.
>
> **Not:** *Due* to traffic, he was tardy.

In the first sentence, *due to traffic* functions as an adjective; in the second sentence, *due to traffic* is a prepositional phrase. Is this giving you a headache? Follow this rule: Don't begin a sentence with *due to*, and you will probably be safe.

**Q: What about *hopefully*?**

**A:** *Hopefully* is an adverb, meaning *in a hopeful manner.* We waited *hopefully* for the lottery numbers to be announced. It's incorrect to use *hopefully* when it doesn't modify a verb: *Hopefully*, the nuclear threat is over. Instead: *It is hoped* that the nuclear threat is over. Sound stilted? You could say *We hope the nuclear threat is over,* or some other variation. (For a while *hopefully* was on the GMAT all the time, but never in the correct answer.)

**Q: Is *percent* singular or plural?**

**A:** It depends. *The percentage* is always singular: *The percentage* of young voters has risen. *A percentage* is singular if the object of the preposition is singular: *A percentage* of the work *is* finished. But *a percentage* is a plural if the object of the preposition is plural: *A percentage* of the reports *are finished.* The same rules apply when using *percent: Sixty percent* of the men *are wearing* hats. *Sixty percent* of the work force *is* absent.

**Q:** Can we go over *affect* and *effect* again?

**A:** Of course! Don't use *affect* as a noun unless you mean it in the psychological sense of *mood*. *Affect* as a verb means *to influence; effect* as a verb means *to bring about, to cause*. So *effect* and *affect* have two distinct meanings—which is partly what is confusing, because you could use either one correctly in the same sentence, although the sentence would then have two different meanings.

He *effected* changes in the corporate structure.

Her shoes *affected* her ability to run.

The weather *affected* my mood.

The weather *effected* tremendous damage along the shore.

His teaching had a poor *effect* on me.

The new drug *effected* his recovery. (brought about his recovery)

The new drug *affected* his recovery. (influenced his recovery—not clear whether the drug helped or hurt his recovery)

**Q:** When a two-part subject is connected by *or*, is it singular or plural?

**A:** It depends. Generally treat the subject as singular, but if you have a singular and a plural subject linked by *or*, make the verb agree with whichever is closer: *The boys or Ralph is eating snails.* And: *Ralph or the boys are eating snails.* The second version sounds better, though both are correct.

# PART 6

# 7 Easy Ways To Look Bad

We did a highly scientific study to determine which grammar mistakes cause the most distress to the listener or reader. In other words, we asked around to find to which grammar mistakes drive people crazy when someone else makes them. Here are the results, in order of degree of irritation caused.

## To Versus Too; Your Versus You're; It's Versus Its

Is it sloppiness, or is it ignorance? *To* is a preposition that indicates direction: I went *to* the dentist. *Your* and *its* are ownership pronouns; use them to indicate possession or ownership: *Your* slip is showing. *You're* and *it's* are contractions, shortened version of *your are* and *it is*. To say *You're slip is showing* would be to say *You are slip is showing,* which would be to sound very silly.

## Between You And I

This is quite common and quite irritating. Remember the trick for dealing with subject and object pronouns: do them one at a time. Between *you.* Correct. Between *I.* Incorrect. Since you would say *between me,* say *between you and me. Me* is the object of the preposition. The reason this error causes listeners such distress is that saying *I* instead of *me* is a sorry attempt to sound stately, or official, or erudite. It is none of these things.

## Lie Versus Lay

This error drives some people crazy, but isn't hard to explain. *Lie* never takes an object; *lie* means *to rest* or *recline*: I need to *lie* down. The books are *lying* on the floor. The principal parts for *lie* are: lie, lay, lying, lain. *Lay* always takes an object, and means *to put down, to place*: He *laid* the books on the floor. He *will lay* himself on a bed of nails. Ask yourself, "Lay what?" In the sentences above, the answer would be *the book* and *himself*. If there is no answer, use *lie*. Strategy number two: if you can substitute *put*, use *lay*. Otherwise use *lie*. The principal parts for *lay* are: lay, laid, laying, laid.

# Bring Or Take?

Use *bring* to indicate movement toward the speaker: *Bring* that book to me. Use *take* to indicate movement away from the speaker: *Take* that book with you when go. Not: I'll *bring* it with me when I go.

# Their Instead Of There

If you make this mistake because you have trouble spelling, you're off the hook. Maybe. Again, is it sloppiness, spelling trouble, or ignorance? You do not want these questions asked about your writing. *There* can be an adverb, a noun, an adjective, or an expletive; *there* indicates location. *Their* is an ownership pronoun: *their pants* means *the pants that belong to them*.

# Infer Or Imply?

When you *infer* something, you are drawing a conclusion or making a deduction: I *infer* from your expression that you are upset. When you *imply* something, you hint—you don't state directly: By standing by the door, I *implied* that it was time for him to leave. You can draw an *inference* from someone else's *implication*, not vice versa.

# Mispronounciations

This isn't exactly grammar. But some mispronunciations can make you sound like an oaf. Don't say heighth for height, nucular for nuclear, and strenth for strength, lenth for length, spaded for spayed, revelant for relevant. When in doubt, look up the pronunciation in the dictionary. Great romances have ended because of repeated violations.

**PART 7**

# Glossary

**absolute adjectives:** adjective that have no comparative or superlative forms because they express a quality you either have or you don't. (*full, perfect, dead*)

**active voice:** use of a verb so that the subject acts directly, as oppose to being acted upon passively. (active: *I smacked him.* passive: *He was smacked by me.*)

**adjective:** a descriptive word that always modifies a noun or pronoun. (*green, pretty, hard*)

**adverb:** a descriptive word that always modifies a verb, adjective, or other adverb. (*quickly, often, sadly*)

**agreement:** subjects and verbs must agree in person and in number. This just means the subject and verb must go together. (*I laugh, he laughs.*) A pronoun must agree with its antecedent. This just means that you must use a singular pronoun if you're referring to a singular noun, and a plural pronoun if you're referring to a plural noun.

**apostrophe:** a punctuation mark that shows ownership (Pinky's puppy) or forms a contraction (don't, wouldn't).

**appositive:** a noun or pronoun, set off by commas, that interrupts the sentence and gives further explanation. (Ralph, *my boss*, was late.)

**article:** a short word that functions as an adjective to indicate *which one*. *The* is the definite article; *a, an* are indefinite articles.

**case:** a category that describes the function of a pronoun: subject, object, or possessive. *He* is the subjective case; *him* is the objective case; *his* is the possessive case.

**clause:** a group of words that has a subject and a verb. Independent clauses may stand alone as a sentence. (*I sneezed today.*) Dependent clauses cannot stand alone. (*While I was walking downtown,* I was hit by a bus.) Clauses can function as nouns, adjectives, or adverbs.

**collective noun:** think of it as a "group" noun. (*committee, jury, family*) Usually treated as singular.

**colon:** a punctuation mark that signals a list to follow, or an explanation. (Three things are needed: a bat, a ball, and a glove.)

**comma:** a punctuation mark used to break up the sentence, to make the reader pause.

**conjunction:** a word the joins words, phrases, or clauses together. Common conjunctions are *and, but, because, yet.*

**continuous:** the six tenses formed by using the *-ing* form of the verb with the regular six tenses. Used to express continuous action, rather than something that happened once and is now over. Also called the progressive tense.

**correlative conjunction:** also known as a **seesaw conjunction**, because it connects equal parts of a sentence together like a seesaw. Common correlative conjunctions are: *not only/but also, either/or, both/and.*

**dangling participle:** a participle that is placed incorrectly in the sentence, so that it modifies the wrong noun. (*Sleeping soundly,* the alarm woke us up.)

**demonstrative pronoun:** also known as **pointing pronouns**. They are used to indicate which thing you are talking about. (*that, these, this, those*)

**dependent clause:** same as **subordinate clause**. A dependent clause is a group of words that has a subject and a verb, but cannot stand alone as a sentence.

**diction:** correct word choice.

**direct object:** a noun receiving the action, not doing the action. (I want to throw *socks*.)

**ellipsis:** an omission, signaled by three dots. Used in quotations, when part of the quote is left out. (He wrote "Man is always attempting...to prove himself.")

**expletive:** a word used as filler or exclamation: *It* is cold out. *Damn!*

**faulty comparison:** an error of clarity. When making a comparison, be sure to compare verb to verb or noun to noun.

**future:** a tense used to describe events that haven't happened yet. Think of it as the "tomorrow" tense. (I *will eat* turkey tomorrow.)

**future perfect:** a combination of a future and past tense, used to show that an action is finished before a specified time in the future. (I *will have finished* the project by next Tuesday.)

**gender:** applies to pronouns; specifies whether the antecedent is male or female.

**gerund:** *-ing* form of the verb, used as a noun. (*Dancing* is fun.)

**hyphen:** a punctuation mark used to form a compound adjective (blue-green, well-born).

**idiom:** a peculiarity of the language; no rules apply. Idioms include figurative language (*raining cats and dogs*) as well as preposition usage. (A slipper is *different from* a boot.)

**imperative mood:** a mood used to boss people around or to give directions. (*Go now.*)

**indefinite pronoun:** a pronoun that doesn't stand in for a specific noun. Examples: *each, either, few, none, plenty.*

**indicative mood:** a mood used to state a fact or ask a question. Most sentences are indicative.

**indirect object:** a substitute for a prepositional phrase. Receiver of the direct object. (Give *me* the cupcake. Direct object = cupcake; indirect object = me.)

**infinitive:** a form of the verb beginning with to. (*to sneeze, to bake*)

**interjection:** an introductory word, often used to show emphasis. *Yikes!* No rules apply!

**interrogative pronoun:** also known as a question pronoun. A pronoun that is used simply to ask a question. *What? Which? Who?*

**intransitive verb:** the distinction between intransitive and transitive verbs is made in the dictionary: *vi* or *vt*, respectively. An intransitive verb doesn't take a direct object. (I walked.) A transitive verb takes a direct object. (She hit the ball.)

**linking conjunction:** also known as a **subordinate conjunction**, this is a conjunction that links a subordinate clause to the rest of the sentence. (*after, while, since, until, if*)

**linking verb:** a verb that doesn't express direct action, but a state of being. (any form of *to be; seem, look, remain*)

**matchmaking conjunctions:** our term for **coordinating conjunctions**. They connect nouns to nouns, phrases to phrases, and clauses to clauses. (*and, but, or, so*)

**misplaced modifier:** often a participial phrase, or any kind of description, that is placed incorrectly in the sentence, so that it appears to modify the wrong thing. Confusion ensues.

**modify:** describe.

**mood:** subjunctive, indicative, and imperative moods are used to describe different types of sentences. See Part 3, Section H for more information on each mood.

**nominative case:** same as subjective case. See **case**.

**noun:** a person, place, thing, quality, or idea. (*toad, anxiety, glee*)

**number:** singular or plural.

**object:** the object of a verb has an action done to it. (She hit *the ball.* She wanted *me.*) The object of a preposition is the noun that finishes the prepositional phrase. (to the *lighthouse,* after the *lecture*)

**objective case:** see **case**.

**parallel construction:** a consideration of syntax. When you make a list, express the elements in the list in similar form, whether they are nouns, phrases, or clauses. Also, when using seesaw (coordinating) conjunctions, express the elements on either side of the conjunction in similar form.

**participle:** the present participle is the *-ing* form of the verb, and goes with *is* (is *asking*). The past participle usually ends in *-ed* and goes with *have* (have *asked*). Without the linking verb (*is, have*) a participle acts as an adjective.

**past tense:** used to express actions that occurred in the past. (I *slept.*)

**past perfect:** a tense used in a sentence that already has a verb in the simple past tense, to express an action that happened even earlier. (Before I slept, I *had eaten* beef.)

**person:** used to categorize personal pronouns. First person: *I, we.* Second person: *you.* Third person: *he, she, they.*

**phrase:** a group of words that can function as a noun, adjective, or adverb. The four main kinds of phrases are prepositional phrases, infinitive phrases, participial phrases, and gerund phrases.

**plural:** more than one, as opposed to singular, which is only one. Applies to nouns, pronouns, and verbs.

**pointing pronoun:** our term for **demonstrative pronoun**. Used to indicate which thing you are talking about. (*That* is crazy.)

**possessive pronoun:** or **ownership pronoun**, shows ownership. (*my, his, their*)

**predicate:** the part of the sentence that is not the subject. Includes the verb and descriptive phrases.

**preposition:** a word showing a relationship of time or space, used to start prepositional phrases. (*to* the floor, *after* the fall)

**present tense:** for now, today. (I *breathe*, he *walks*)

**present perfect:** a tense used to express action that started in the past and continues into the present, or was finished at some earlier time but still affects the present situation. (She *has slept* for hours; I am upset because I *have lost* my mittens.)

**principal parts:** basic verb forms including present, past, present participle, and past participle.

**progressive:** *-ing* tense, same as **continuous**.

**pronoun:** a word that stands in for a noun. There are several classes of pronouns: personal (*she, it*); relative (*that, which*); interrogative or question (*what, which*); indefinite (*both, each, any, many*); demonstrative (*these, those*); reflexive or mirror (*itself, yourself, themselves*).

**question pronoun:** or **interrogative pronoun**, is used to ask a question: *What? Who?*

**redundancy:** saying the same thing twice; needless repetition. (*close proximity*)

**reflexive pronoun:** or **mirror pronoun**, is used to spin the action back at the subject (He loves only *himself.*), or for emphasis. (The candidate *himself* wrote the speech.)

**relative clause:** a subordinate, or dependent, clause that is introduced by a relative pronoun (*which, that, who, what*). A relative clause always acts as an adjective.

**relative pronoun:** introduces a relative clause. Examples: *which, that, who*. Indefinite relative pronouns have no antecedent. (*what, which, whatever, whomever*)

**seesaw conjunction:** our term for **correlative conjunctions.** Examples include: *either/or, both/and, neither/nor, not only/but also.* Parts on either side of a seesaw conjunction must be matched in form.

**semicolon:** a punctuation mark used to separate two independent clauses. (I ran; I fell.)

**singular:** used to describe nouns and pronouns when there is only one of them (*bus, it*) as opposed to plural, more than one. Also used to describe the verb form that matches the singular noun or pronoun (bus *moves,* it *flies*).

**subject:** the main noun of the sentence (the noun that does the action), along with any words or phrases that modify the main noun. (*She* walks.)

**subjunctive mood:** used in statements that are contrary to fact, or in *that* clauses of order or recommendation.

**subordinate clause:** also known as a **dependent clause**, this is a clause that can't stand alone as a sentence. It will be introduced by a linking, or subordinate conjunction (*after, while, if*) or a relative pronoun (*which, that, who*).

**subordinating conjunction:** also known as **linking conjunctions**. They introduce a subordinate, or dependent, clause. Examples of subordinating conjunctions include: *after, if, while.*

**tense:** a form of the verb that tells what time the action happened. There are twelve tenses altogether: present, present perfect, past, past perfect, future, future perfect; and the continuous (or progressive) forms of these six.

**transitive verb:** takes a direct object (She *hit me*) as opposed to an intransitive verb, which doesn't (She *swam*). See **intransitive verb**.

**verbal:** a phrase that looks like a verb but performs a different function in the sentence. The three kinds of verbals are infinitives, gerunds, and participles. They can act as nouns, adjectives, or adverbs.

# PART 8

# The World Series

It's all here: parts of speech, parts of the sentence, tense, parallel construction, misplaced modifiers, faulty comparisons, idioms, diction, redundancy, voice and mood, agreement. If you find yourself repeatedly missing questions on a particular subject, then by all means, go back and review.

# Quiz #1:

*In parentheses at the end of each sentence you are given a part of speech. In the blanks, write in the appropriate form of that part of speech. There may be more than one correct answer; you need to write in only one of them.*

1. Dinosaurs _____ the earth for more than 100 million years before becoming extinct. (*verb: to roam*)

2. In the badlands of Montana paleontologists have discovered dinosaur nests as well as fossils different _____ those found at other sites. (*preposition*)

3. There _____, according to any paleontologist you might ask, myriad controversies about the behavior and even the physical appearance of most dinosaurs. (*verb: to be*)

4. The small boys, one of _____ was an expert on dinosaurs, were thrilled to go on a trip to the museum of natural history. (*relative pronoun*)

5. The boys took pictures of the giant fossil skeletons, quizzed each other on the names of obscure reptiles, and _____ a riot in the cafeteria. (*verb: to cause*)

# Quiz #2

## Pick One

*You've got two choices. Pick the correct one.*

1. Rhonda woke up one morning to find herself afflicted (by, with) mumps.

2. (Her, She) and her brother Maximilian had to drink soup through straws because mumps made eating impossible.

3. "If I (were, was) you, I would not look in the mirror," said Maximilian.

4. "I am totally (disinterested in, indifferent to) anything you have to say, Fatface," answered Rhonda.

5. The period of convalescence, (which, that) lasted over a week, gave Rhonda and Maximilian enough time to get tired of fighting with each other.

# Quiz #3:

## Error ID

*Circle the underlined error, or circle E if there is no error.*

1. While getting <u>ready for</u> the Halloween party, <u>the hot water</u> ran
                A                            B

   out and Mindy <u>was forced</u> <u>to take</u> a sponge bath with cold
                    C        D

   water. _____
       E

2. <u>Although she had</u> worked <u>hard</u> on her costume, she was worried
        A                B

   that the other celebrants <u>might have</u> better costumes than <u>her</u>.
                       C                            D

   _____
   E

3. The reason Mindy <u>decided to dress</u> as a <u>tomato</u> was <u>because</u> her
                     A             B         C

   favorite food <u>was</u> spaghetti with marinara sauce. _____
              D                              E

4. <u>In fact</u>, Mindy refused to eat <u>anything else</u>, and even her
    A

   career decision <u>was marked with</u> her tomato sauce obsession; she
                      C

   <u>planned for being</u> head chef at an Italian restaurant. _____
        D                                       E

5. She imagined <u>that she would</u> cook tomato sauce
                     A

   <u>for thousands, even millions</u>, of grateful diners, and that
               B

   she <u>would become known</u> as one of the most <u>imminent</u>
             C                                  D

   Italian chefs in the world. _____
                          E

# Quiz #4:

## Match It

*Match the correct pronoun from the list at the bottom. Don't use any pronoun more than once, and some pronouns won't be used at all.*

1. The beautiful actress, _____ we have seen perform on stage as well as in movies, has gotten _____ a facelift.

2. All members of the audience believe _____, and no one else, understands the true depth of her performance.

3. During the late show, all the theater-goers took _____ seats long before the lights were dimmed.

4. The many years of study, _____ she paid for by working menial jobs, finally paid off when the actress got her first lead role.

5. The actress was beloved by others _____ worked in the industry, because she never ignored _____ who had helped her along the way.

| | | | |
|---|---|---|---|
| a. whatever | e. who | i. themselves | m. herself |
| b. whomever | f. her (or his) | j. each | n whichever |
| c. those | g. himself | k. whom | o. them |
| d. their | h. that | l. they | p. which |

# Quiz #5:

## Q&A

1. What's the rule for subject-verb agreement?

_____

2. What does a gerund look like?

_____

3. What part of speech does a gerund function as?

_____

4. What parts of speech do adverbs modify?

_____

5. What are collective nouns, and what do you have to remember about them?

_____

6. What are the two situations in which to use the subjunctive?

_____

# Quiz #6:

## Phrase Substitution

*Pick the best answer.*

1. Succeeding at a career in the arts—whether literature, fine arts, or theater—is more difficult <u>succeeding</u> in business.

    A) than succeeding

    B) than success

    C) than success is

    D) from succeeding

    E) from success

2. <u>One should avoid eating excessive amounts</u> of fat, especially animal fat, if you want to stay fit and healthy.

    A) One should avoid eating excessive amounts

    B) One should avoid the eating of an excessive amount

    C) One should, by avoiding eating excessive quantities

    D) You should avoid eating excessive amounts

    E) You should have an avoidance to eating excessive quantities

3. The reason thousands of young people come to live in New York City every year <u>is because New York offers</u> the chance to realize ambitions in nearly every sphere, whether in the arts or in business.

    A) is because New York offers

    B) is that New York offers

    C) being that New York can offer

    D) are that New York is offering

    E) are because New York offers

4. <u>Like James Joyce</u>, Henry James worked to develop a literary style that rendered reality in an unprecedented way.

   A) Like James Joyce

   B) As for James Joyce

   C) As did James Joyce

   D) Similar to James Joyce

   E) Similarly to James Joyce

5. The study of economics, both micro and macro, <u>are necessary to understanding</u> political science.

   A) are necessary to understanding

   B) are necessary in the understanding of

   C) is necessary for understanding

   D) is a necessity in the understanding of

   E) is necessary to understanding

# Quiz #7:

## Fix It

*Correct the following sentences.*

1. The purpose of art is not to instruct, but allowing a person to experience an emotional response to the work.

2. Serious political discussion are better left to essays and speeches, where arguments can be developed and objections raised and commented upon.

3. Nevertheless, you can easily think of many masterpieces, like Picasso's *Guernica,* which demand that you consider the political event that inspired it.

4. Writers who I consider among my favorites have never written directly about politics, although I could argue that a political ethic underlies their work.

5. Rather than comply to some so-called politically correct notion of what art should be about, the artists I most admire create their work from their own obsessions, which may or may not be political.

# Quiz #8:

## Match It

*The following sentence fragments invite certain grammatical errors. Match the fragment with the error that you would need to watch out for. (This quiz is especially useful if you plan to take the SAT II: Writing and the GMAT.)*

1. Among the many reasons for his failure were...

2. Unlike transistor radios...

3. The reason the world is falling apart...

4. When one plants a garden...

5. Exhausted from undressing...

a. faulty comparison     e. subject-verb agreement

b. pronoun agreement     f. misplaced modifier

c. subjunctive mood     g. passive/active voice

d. parallel construction     h. redundancy

# Quiz #9:

## Pick One

*You've got two choices. Pick the correct one.*

1. We will, (hopefully, it is hoped), someday live in a city that takes care of its poor.

2. What is wrong with (my, me) coming to dinner early?

3. The writer's new book has been bought by a stupendous (amount, number) of readers, none of whom will actually read the book.

4. The lottery jackpot was divided (among, between) the four cousins, who had combined their birthdays for their winning numbers.

5. Pinky, along with Ralphie and Gomez, (are, is) asleep on the sofa under a pile of newspapers.

# Quiz #10:

## Q&A

1. What's the rule for parallel construction?

_____

2. When would you use _fewer_, and when would you use _less_?

_____

3. What's the difference between _ambiguous_ and _ambivalent_?

_____

4. What is redundancy?

_____

5. How do you find the subject of a sentence?

_____

# Quiz #11:

## Jeopardy!

*Listed below are answers—you give the questions. Remember to phrase your question as "What is..." or "What are..." just like on* Jeopardy. *The category is Parts of Speech.*

1. only, roughly, often, insidiously

_____

2. but, because, if, yet

_____

3. death, sex, glory, denial

_____

4. Wow! Ha! Ouch! Oof!

_____

5. in, at, with, to

_____

# Quiz #12:

## Error Identification

*Pick the error. If there isn't an error, pick E.*

1. If Roscoe <u>would have bothered</u> to look out the window, he
   <br>A

   <u>would have seen</u> his car <u>being pummeled</u> by hailstones <u>as big as</u>
   <br>B                 C                           D

   baseballs. _____
   <br>      E

2. <u>Due to the fact that</u> Roscoe <u>had just bought his</u> car, he was
   <br>     A                             B

   <u>disconsolate</u> over the damage the hailstorm <u>had caused</u>. _____
   <br>   C                                   D     E

3. If <u>I was</u> Roscoe, I <u>would hammer</u> even <u>more</u> dents into the car, and
   <br>   A               B             C

   turn <u>the battered vehicle</u> into artwork. _____
   <br>     D                     E

4. <u>Having watched</u> his precious car be subjected to the fury of nature,
   <br>   A

   Roscoe began to show symptoms of psychosis, <u>such as believing</u>
   <br>                                             B

   the hailstones were a physical manifestation of every sin

   <u>he had ever</u> committed, and singing to himself to drown
   <br>   C

   out the voices he <u>continually</u> heard speaking to him. _____
   <br>                    D                       E

5. The <u>principal</u> lesson <u>to be learned</u> from Roscoe's sad experience is
   <br>     A             B

   <u>that one</u> should not become too attached to <u>one's</u> material belong-
   <br>   C                                     D

   ings. _____
   <br>  E

# Quiz #13:

## Mark It

*The following sentence need punctuating. Go for it.*

1. Before eating Mindy packed four items for her trip a mousetrap a hairbrush a mug in the shape of a duck and a canned ham

2. Canned ham was Mindys favorite food she ate it as least once a day usually washing it down with a root beer float

3. I can't wait to leave for Costa Rica shouted Mindy clutching her guidebook under her arm and doing a jig

4. Costa Rica which is west of Panama is extremely mountainous Mindy had packed hiking gear along with a couple of extra canned hams for emergencies on the trail

5. Mindy said that it was entirely possible that her life could be saved by a canned ham if she found herself lost in the rainforest with no knowledge of which plants were edible

# Quiz #14:

## Fill-ins

*Fill in each blank with the correct preposition.*

1. If you tamper _____ the lawn mower, the blade may fly off and now somebody down.

2. Lawn mowers, in the advertising fantasies of the suburbs, are depicted _____ useful practicalities, but in fact, they are ear-splitting machines of destruction.

3. If you are in search _____ a way to cut your grass, consider buying a grazing animal or using a manual lawn mower.

4. One big advantage of grazing animals, which makes them superior _____ other methods of lawn management, is that they provide their own high-quality fertilizer at absolutely no cost to the owner.

5. Total dependence of the suburbanite _____ machines that run on fossil fuels results _____ a life not quite so carefree, or guilt-free, as the sitcoms of the 1950s would lead us to believe.

# Quiz #15:

## Phrase Substitution

*Pick the best answer.*

1. <u>During the presidency of George Bush, the economy went into a recession, and it</u> made his reelection highly unlikely, no matter what other issues were raised.

   A) During the presidency of George Bush, the economy went into a recession, and it

   B) The presidency of George Bush, during which the economy went into a recession,

   C) While George Bush was the president, the economy went into a recession, and

   D) The recession of the economy that occurred during the presidency of George Bush

   E) The economy's going into recession during the presidency of George Bush

2. After buying an apartment during the real estate boom of the eighties, the couple hoped <u>it would make further investments for their financial security unnecessary</u>.

   A) it would make further investments for their financial security unnecessary

   B) they would, for their financial security, not necessarily need to make further investments

   C) that the purchase would make further investments for their financial security unnecessary

   D) that, having made the purchase, they would then have no necessity for making further investments for their financial security

   E) further investments for their financial securer will be unnecessary

3. Although the great blizzard seemed to hit it the hardest, Mootown was really just one of many towns in the path of the storm that <u>was without electricity and phone service for nearly a week</u>.

   A) was without electricity and phone service for nearly a week

   B) was without both electricity and phone service for almost a week

   C) being without both electricity and phone service for close to a week

   D) were without electricity, as well as phone service, for upwards of a week

   E) were without electricity and phone service for nearly a week

4. Because whales do not feed on creatures high on the food chain, <u>as sharks do</u>, they must consume mind-boggling quantities of their preferred food, which is known as krill.

A) as sharks do

B) as does a shark

C) like a shark

D) like sharks

E) unlike sharks

5. The economic advisers recommend <u>that interest rates will not be changed</u> until the next fiscal year.

A) that interest rates will not be changed

B) that interest rates not be changed

C) interest rates not to change

D) no changing of the rates of interest

E) interest rates to not change

# Quiz #16:

## Q&A

1. What's the difference between *effect* and *affect?*

_____

2. What's the rule for *among* and *between?*

_____

3. When is it correct to begin a sentence with *because?*

_____

4. What is the difference between *compare to* and *compare with?*

_____

5. What is the difference between a *phrase* and a *clause?*

_____

# Quiz #17:

## Pick One

*You've got two choices. Pick the better one.*

1. When green slime started to ooze from the newscaster's ear, the audience was horrified and (nauseated, nauseous).

2. (Like, As do) humans, dogs and cats enjoy spending some part of their day playing.

3. The lizard (lies, lays) on the rock and closes his beady eyes.

4. It was (he, him) who won the prize.

5. In 1902, my grandmother, dressed in petticoats and a fur hat, (has been, was) arrested and thrown in jail.

# Quiz #18:

## Fix It

*The following sentences may have an error or two, or even three. Or they may be correct. Fix them if necessary.*

1. One of the first things to find out, when starting a new job, are the location of the coffee machine, where employees gather to spread rumors and complain about the boss.

2. It seems to be true that there is always one loudmouth in every workplace, who attempts to take credit for any innovation and never takes the blame for screw-ups.

3. Among the reasons Buffy quit her job were that she was bored, that she had no further chance of promotion, and she had a better offer in another city.

4. Wandering aimlessly through the city, there were several tragic events that the writer witnessed and recorded in her notebook.

5. The boss sent a memo to Buffy and I, recommending that we should be on time to work.

# Quiz #19:

## Jeopardy!

*Hey! It's TV time again. Phrase your answer in the "What is..." or "What are..." format. The category is Parts of the Sentence, including phrases (gerund, prepositional, participial, infinitive) and clauses (noun, adjective, adverb). Focus on the italicized part of the sentence and identify the part of the sentence.*

1. After her long trip, Zippy had a difficult time readjusting *to her daily life.*

   _____

2. One day in the shower she noticed *that her leg were covered with red spots.*

   _____

3. *Scrubbing the spots vigorously,* Zippy wondered if she had parasites, and if so, whether the parasites were fatal.

   _____

4. Wanting to set her mind at ease, she called her friend Nippy, *who was a respected doctor at the local hospital.*

   _____

5. Maybe *eating the local food without taking any precautions* was a bad idea.

   _____

# Quiz #20:

## Match It

*Using the following sentences, match each verb, in List B, with its subject, in List A. List A includes some words that aren't subjects. Ignore them.*

1. Wanda is one of the millions of women who dye their eyebrows.

2. Frogs, which are amphibians, have a variety of defenses to ward off predators.

3. Zippy's favorite food, no matter what season it is, happens to be chili.

4. After walking all the way downtown, Buffy and her friends realized they had forgotten their shoes.

5. Driving without a license is one way to get a ticket.

| List A | | List B |
|---|---|---|
| a. Wanda | j. season | a. is |
| b. one | k. downtown | b. dye |
| c. millions | l. Buffy and her friends | c. are |
| d. Frogs | m. they | d. have |
| e. which | n. shoes | e. is |
| f. amphibians | o. Driving | f. happens to be |
| g. variety | p. license | g. realized |
| h. Zippy's favorite | q. one | h. had forgotten |
| i. food | r. ticket | i. is |

# Quiz #21:

## Error ID

*Circle the error. If there isn't an error, circle E.*

1. Before <u>he</u> left for college, Frankie picked up his paycheck <u>and said</u>
   A                                                                    B
   goodbye to his girlfriend, and <u>with great</u> eagerness <u>was packing</u> his
                                        C                          D
   car for the long drive. _____
                            E

2. Although maintaining barely a C average in high school, the

   <u>expectation</u> Frankie had was to earn straight As in college, <u>since</u>
   A                                                                   B
   he <u>would be able</u> to study <u>what</u> interested him. _____
        C                        D                         E

3. Our English teacher wanted Frankie and <u>I</u> to major in English
                                            A
   <u>so that</u> we could spend our college days curled up in armchairs
   B
   reading novels, <u>which</u> certainly sounded better <u>than working</u> all
                    C                                    D
   day in a chemistry lab. _____
                           E

4. Frankie and <u>I</u> liked reading everything from comic books to
                 A
   Russian novels; <u>whatever</u> the librarian gave us, we read quickly,
                    B
   <u>even if</u> that <u>meant</u> not doing any of our homework. _____
   C              D                                            E

5. Frankie <u>had convinced</u> the admissions committee that he would
               A
   study hard once he got to college; <u>nevertheless</u>, his hobbies
                                        B
   <u>ranged from</u> herpetology to furniture design, and he did not plan
   C
   on giving any of <u>them</u> up to make time for studying. _____
                     D                                        E

# Quiz #22:

## Pick One

*Again, two choices. Pick the correct one.*

1. If, after seeing the photographs, Ronald (had, would have) contacted the police, possibly he would not now be awaiting trial in the city jail.

2. In his deposition, Ronald made an (allusion, illusion) to Ezra Pound.

3. Ronald was one of the criminals who (claim, claims) innocence no matter how convincing the evidence against them might be.

4. Mercy was what, in his testimony, he asked (of, from) the jury.

5. While he waited for the jury to reach (its, their) verdict, Ronald saw the photograph on the stack of papers on the table in front of his lawyers, and wondered whether (it, they) might be able to save him.

# Quiz #23:

## Jeopardy!

*Each of the following sentences has an error. Your question should identify it. Example: He are here. What is subject-verb agreement?*

1. Winky, who was hard of hearing, loves geraniums more than Zippy.

   _____

2. Zippy's favorite thing was socks; and he particularly loved socks that had a floral design and reinforced toes.

   _____

3. Although they had paid for the tickets and packed for the long trip, Zippy was still worried about trailing with Winky, because they had never been able to cooperate together.

   _____

4. Irregardless of whether the weather was hot, Zippy wore socks, much to the dismay of Winky, who had an enviable sense of fashion.

   _____

5. Dragging his massive suitcase toward the elevator, Winky's passport was still lying on the table in the hallway instead of being tucked away in a safe place for traveling.

   _____

# Quiz #24:

## Q&A

1. When do you use *lie*, and when do you use *lay?*

_____

2. When do you use *bring*, and when do you use *take?*

_____

3. What's a split infinitive?

_____

4. What's the difference between *infer* and *imply?*

_____

5. What's the rule for using hyphens with compound adjectives?

_____

# Quiz #25:

## You're on Your Own

1. Write a sentence with a comparison, making sure it isn't a faulty comparison.

_____

_____

2. Write a sentence using correct parallel construction.

_____

_____

3. Write a sentence using at least three pronouns, Make sure to watch out for agreement, case, and ambiguity.

_____

_____

4. Write a sentence that begins with a modifying phrase, and make sure it isn't a misplaced modifier.

_____

_____

5. Write a sentence with two independent clauses joined by a semi-colon. Make sure your subjects and verb agree.

_____

_____

# Answer Key

## QQ #1: Identifying Nouns

Zach Morris, Casey Jones, hosts, showcase, Blast Masters Club, musicians, area, they, instruments, Zach, Casey, banter, musicians, cream of the crop, headliner, lady, stage name, Tooth Fairy, she, rocker, New York City, she, Big Apple, She, Zach, Casey, years, they, Sundays, diner, minutes, club

## QQ #2: More Nouns

1. aliens (plural); Subaru (singular, proper); juice (singular)

2. committee (singular, collective); decorations (plural); prom (singular)

3. lunch (singular); bacteria (plural)

4. Swimming (singular)

5. Wednesday (singular, proper); Wanda (singular, proper); Wichita (singular, proper); Wilbur (singular, proper)

## QQ #3: Billy Wifflamoo, The Birth

dark, his, loving, hospital, jagged, bad, balding, superstitious, balding, scary, young, Billy's, brand-new, newborn, newborn, his, normal, his, green, bloody, any, other, perceptive, other, subtle, weirder, average

(Notice that some of these adjectives could perform other functions—*hospital* could be a noun, for instance. *Any* and *other* could be pronouns. A word does not necessarily have a fixed part of speech—the part of speech depends on how it is used in the sentence.)

## QQ #4: Identifying Adjectives

6. fewer (individual marshmallows)

7. a perfect (absolute adjective)

8. better (comparing two things)

9. spongier than (comparing marshmallow to any other single food: two things)

10. many (individual marshmallows); less (uncountable Jell-O)

## QQ #5: Are You Tense?

There are several correct answers for some questions in this drill. If you wrote in any of the following you are A-Okay:

1. waits, is waiting, waited, was waiting, has waited, has been waiting

2. screamed, was screaming; forgot, had forgotten

3. will give

4. had remembered

5. will have, will be having

## QQ #6: Principal Parts

1. drunk

2. laid, wept

3. hanged

4. sworn

5. lain

## QQ #7: Billy Wifflamoo, The Early Years

loudly, often, later, fondly, almost, ever, Quickly, quietly, well, enough, only, extremely

## QQ #8: Personal Pronouns

1. me

2. me

3. I

4. I (to mean "the hairdresser liked my hair more than I did") me (to mean "the hairdresser liked my hair more than he liked me"). So either I or me is correct—but they give the sentence different meanings.

## QQ #9: Relative Pronouns

1. that; that

2. who

3. whom

4. which

5. that

## QQ #10: Billy Wifflamoo, Aliens Ate My Buick

most, many, none, each, all, anything, nothing, one another, everything, all, anything

## QQ #11: Billy Wifflamoo, The Teen Years

at school, into cliques, of none, of them, in his own clique, in itself, by definition, in fact, for something, in some hidden way, for a visit, from the alien

## QQ #12: Identifying Conjunctions

1. (bathing) and (shaving)

2. (He was obsessed with cleanliness) but (his closet was a mess)

3. not only (took four showers a day) but also (washed his clothes twice)

4. either (afraid of germs) or (afraid of looking unkempt)

5. (yesterday) and (today)

## QQ #13: More On Identifying Conjunctions

1. Reginald was late to work [because he washed his hair 16 times.]

2. [Since his boss was also obsessed with cleanliness,] Reginald was not reprimanded for being late.

3. Reginald will not have much of a social life [as long as he considers everyone too cavalier regarding hygiene.]

4. [Until he cleans that messy closet,] he will not sleep well at night.

5. Reginald is obsessed with filth [because he does not want to think about anything else.]

## QQ #14: Parts Of Speech

Since you made up your own words for this drill, we can't really give you an answer key. Look your words up in the dictionary to check parts of speech; remember that some words can have as many as four different parts of speech, depending on the usage. Below is just an example.

**NOUNS:**

1. socks

2. happiness

3. acorns

4. trout

5. hair

**ADJECTIVES:**

1. new socks

2. abundant happiness

3. green acorns

4. smoked trout

5. long hair

**CORRECT PRONOUN:**

1. they

2. it

3. they

4. it or they

5. it

**PREPOSITIONAL PHRASES:**

1. under the new socks

2. with abundant happiness

3. in green acorns

4. after smoked trout

5. of long hair

**VERBS:**

1. swim

2. was dancing

3. kiss

4. am concentrating

5. be

**ADVERBS:**

1. swim quickly

2. was dancing crazily

3. softly kiss

4. am concentrating deeply

5. always be

# Batting Practice, Part 1

## Drill 1

1. **E.** *Unique* is an absolute adjective; you can't be more or less unique. That gets rid of A, B, and C. Choice D uses the past perfect continuous (*had been designing*) for no good reason. Past perfect is more appropriate because it makes clear that the dress was designed at an earlier time than Gomez thought.

2. **D.** *That* is better than *which*, because the clause *that were made for Pinky and me* defines which dresses we mean. Also, the clause is not set off by commas, which is another indicator that *which* would not be appropriate. That eliminates A and B. In C, the clause *having been made* functions as an adjective, leaving the sentence with no verb. Also in A and C the pronoun case is incorrect: made for *me*, not made for *I*. Choice E is awkward and uses *hanged*, which only applies to people (grotesquely enough), not dresses.

3. **D.** *Criteria* is plural; *criterion* is singular. So A, B, and E are out. C switches from *you* to *one*. Remember to keep pronouns consistent.

4. **C.** *Amount* applies to noncountable nouns, such as water. Cross out A, B, and D. E has a tense problem; the sentence is referring to 1978, so you need past tense (*wore*), not present continuous (*are wearing*).

5. **C.** Look at the clause *but her and me have*: the verb *have* requires a subject, so *her* or *me* (objective case) is incorrect. Get rid of A, B, and E. D says *are being back*, which is nutty. Also, pumps and tight jeans are countable nouns, so *fewer* is appropriate, not *less*.

# Drill 2

1. **A.** When comparing two nouns, use the comparative form: *more talented*. *Most talented* is the superlative form, used to compare more than two nouns.

2. **C.** Wrong principal part. The past participle of *begin* is *begun*.

3. **E.** No problem.

4. **A.** Use *among* for more than two; *between* for two.

5. **C.** *Constant* is an adjective. The word being modified is *changing*, a verb, so we need an adverb: *constantly*.

# Drill 3

1. I     am     shivering     from     the     cold.
   PRO   VERB   VERB          PREP     ART     NOUN

2. I     made     delicious     pot roast     and
   PRO   VERB     ADJ           NOUN          CONJ

   beans     and     rice     for     dinner.
   NOUN      CONJ    NOUN     PREP    NOUN

3. There     is     nothing     better     than     pot roast,
   PRO       VERB   PRO         ADJ        PREP     NOUN

   in     my     opinion.
   PREP   PRO    NOUN

4. Yikes!     I     somehow     left     my     hat
   INTERJ     PRO   ADV         VERB     ADJ    NOUN

   in     the     oven!
   PREP   ART     NOUN

5. Actually,    we      would      rather     order  Chinese
   ADV          PRO     VERB       ADV        VERB   ADJ

   food         and     watch      TV,
   NOUN         CONJ    VERB       NOUN

   because      we      can        eat        these
   CONJ         PRO     VERB       VERB       ADJ

   fortune cookies      and        stand      on     our
   NOUN                 CONJ       VERB       PREP   ADJ

   heads        until   we         are        ready  for     bed.
   NOUN         CONJ    PRO        VERB       ADJ    PREP    NOUN

NOTE: Pot roast and fortune cookies may be thought of as one noun.

## QQ #15:Finding The Subject

1. Oscar

2. You (Note that this is implied. The entire sentence would be *You, don't walk on the grass.*)

3. Who

4. socks

5. roommates

## QQ #16: Billy Wifflamoo, Teen Love Idol

There came a moment (and a short moment it was) when Billy was the primary love object of all the girls in his school. Girls had been falling for the best-looking, most athletic, most charming boys, but one day, Billy had something none of them had: he had actual contact with an alien. This made him famous and much admired.

The alien had touched Billy's ear with his spiky green finger. Billy's ear had swelled to six times the normal size for ears, and he was suddenly able to hear very acutely. He could hear what his neighbors were saying in their living room, which was not at all interesting. The alien touched all of Billy's body parts, and in turn, each grew to six times its normal size. Soon Billy himself was a pretty big guy. The alien taught Billy how to do this for himself, whenever he felt like it. He performed this trick at school, which was why the girls fell in love with him. It didn't last.

After Billy shrank back to normal size, he and the alien talked about baseball. The alien liked the Red Sox, a doomed team if ever there was one.

## QQ #17: Identifying the Predicate

1. (Bob) has six toes on his left foot.

2. Embarrassed, and tired of being the butt of jokes, (he) resolved never to take off his shoes.

3. After pleading with Bob for years, (his parents) finally persuaded him to see a plastic surgeon.

4. "Not everybody is so lucky," said (the surgeon) when he saw Bob's toes.

## QQ #18: Finding Direct And Indirect Objects

1. The mother hid (the matches) in a drawer.

2. The child found (the matches) and started (a bonfire) in the living room.

3. The fireman gave the boy a (bucket) of water.

4. As the flames leapt higher the boy threw (himself) on the ground and cried.

5. Later the mother bought him a new toy (fire truck) and then told him the (story) of Prometheus.

## QQ #19: Finding Prepositional Phrases

1. In a huff; to the party

2. in a new suit; in the crowd

3. of the partygoers; on their hands

4. across the room

5. Beyond the kissing couple; with a pile; of socks; under the table; of CDs

## QQ #20: Finding Infinitives

1. to scream

2. to be told (*to her friend* is a prepositional phrase)

3. to know

4. To have been; to have suffered

5. to find; to hold

## QQ #21: Finding Gerunds

1. cleaning

2. Partying; talking on the phone

3. hiring someone; spending money

## QQ #22: Identifying Participial Phrases

1. Walking quickly to work

2. Too tired to turn back

3. covered with piles of papers and phone messages

4. Throwing himself into his work

5. Laughing and pointing

## QQ #23: Identifying Dependent Clauses

1. (When the party was assembled at the table) → adverb clause

2. (which was scheduled to take place at midnight) → adjective clause

3. (What made the couple so uncertain) → noun clause

4. (Because the wedding was to be held at midnight) → adverb clause

5. (After they had eaten) → adverb clause

## QQ #24: Subject-Verb Olympics

(the subject is in parentheses)

1. (Bob) was

2. (Bob) is

3. (Many) are

4. (danger) does

5. (dangers) do

## QQ #25: Subject-Verb Olympics

1. (Bob and Harry) look

2. (Dick) is yearning

3. (Either) (Dick) wants

4. (Neither) (Bob) desires

5. (Neither) (boys) desire

In 3, 4, and 5 the verb agrees with the noun closest to it.

## QQ #26: Subject-Verb Olympics

1. (Each) is

2. (family) is; (anything) is

3. (men) are

4. (Everyone) comes; sees; have

5. (one) has; (Committee) has

## QQ #27: Pronoun Agreement

1. In an election year, many of the candidates abandon their usual causes and talk instead about any issue they think will get them elected.

2. Unfortunately, a campaign manager will do virtually anything, legal or not, to ensure his or her candidate's reelection.

3. Each of the voters makes his or her own decision. Or: All of the voters make their own decisions.

4. Everyone in the campaign office has, at one time or another, offered a suggestion for an advertisement that would severely damage the opposing candidate's credibility, but each person has since retracted his or her suggestion, fearing that such an advertisement would invite attacks on his or her own candidate's credibility.

   NOTE: See Part 3 Section I for tips on gender-neutral writing.

5. No error.

## QQ #28: Parallel Construction

1. **E**. The list is: *writing, managing, planning,* and *analyzing.* Four gerunds. C and D say *to manage* instead of *managing*; A says *to plan* instead of *planning*; B sticks the preposition *for* where it doesn't belong.

2. **D**. What is parallel here is *spring* and *developed: did not spring...but developed.* A and B put the *not* in the wrong place, and set up an expectation that her suspicion sprang not from an incident but from something else. C uses the continuous tense for no good reason. E isn't parallel: *did not spring...but was developing.* This is a difficult question.

3. **B**. The list is: *to sneak, to go, to communicate, to plan.* Four infinitives. A, C, and D say *planning* instead of *plan*; D and E say *communicating* instead of *to communicate.*

4. **B**. The list is: *that* she would be; *that* she would figure; and *that* she would earn. Three *that* clauses. A, C, D, and E fail to say *that* she would figure, so none of them are parallel.

5. **A**. Ha! Trick question. She decided (1) to research (2) to make friends. Two infinitives, but both have dependent clauses that make it easy to lose your sense of the structure of the sentence. *By bugging his phone* is a modifying phrase within the *which* clause; it is not on the structural list of the sentence. This is a good example of a difficult GMAT question.

## QQ #29: Misplaced Modifiers

1. **D**. What was nearly completed? Not *the analysts* but *the report*. A, B, C, and E all make the same mistake. In D, *it* must refer to *report*, because *report* is singular; *it* can't refer to *analysts*, because *analysts* is plural.

2. **B**. Bob was not added to the raise and a company car. But Bob demanded a four-day work week in addition to the raise and a company car. In A the modifier is misplaced. E is not parallel: *to the raise* and *wanted*. C and D don't make much sense.

3. **E**. Who was mowing the many-acred lawn? Bob, not the skies. The modifier is misplaced in A and B. C has the vulgar *being as*, which is never correct. D is awkward because *the skies darkening* is stuck into the sentence without a conjunction or preposition to clarify its relation to the sentence.

4. **C**. Who was depressed and sorrowfully inadequate? Bob, or a pronoun standing for Bob, not the job. The modifier is misplaced in A, B, and E. D says *being that*, which you should wipe out of your vocabulary; it is never correct.

5. **C**. Who stocked up on Doritos? Bob, so Bob must follow the comma. A, B, and E have misplaced modifiers. D is unidiomatic (preferring...over) and otherwise atrocious.

## QQ #30: Fixing Faulty Comparisons

1. Unlike mushrooms and other fungi, tomatoes are cultivated in as much sun as possible. Or: We cultivate tomatoes, unlike mushrooms and fungi, in as much sun as possible.

2. At the state fair, Pinky's tomatoes won more prizes than Bob's did.

3. No error.

4. Pinky had done more research on organic gardening that Bob had.

## QQ #31: Idioms

1. different **from**

2. afflicted **with**

3. prohibited **from buying**

4. Compared **with**

5. dispute **over**

## QQ #32: Diction

1. emigrated should be changed to immigrated

2. You immigrate to, emigrate from

3. incredulous should be changed to incredible

4. immanent should be changed to eminent

5. principle should be changed to principal

6. respectively should be changed to respectfully

7. sensory should be changed to sensual

8. disinterested should be changed to uninterested or not interested

9. alternates should be changed to alternatives

# Batting Practice, Part 3

## Drill 1

1. **D**. A and B make incomplete comparisons. *As great as or greater than* is correct, but better, and shorter, is *at least as great as*. C says *than that of* instead of *that brought about by*, which means the sentence would be saying insufficient rest's stress, overwork's stress, poor diet's stress, all of which is awkward and false. E isn't parallel: through resting...and overwork.

2. **B**. A says *where* instead of *in which*; use *where* only to talk about a geographical place. A and E violate subject-verb agreement by saying *collectives...which provides*. C and D also violate agreement. C starts with *a dairy farmer* and then says *their*; D is plural until the very end, when it says *the farmer*.

3. **B**. The list is: *herding, warning, acting*. A and E aren't parallel. C, D, and E use *like* instead of *such as*. C and E violate pronoun agreement by saying *its*. D violates agreement by going from plural *dogs* to singular *a herder*.

4. **C**. A, B, and E make faulty comparisons: buying stocks to an investor, buying stocks to an investment. D is closer, but still makes a faulty comparison; better would be *When buying stocks* to *when investing*. D also misplaces *directly*—put adverbs next to the word being modified.

5. **E**. A, B, and C don't use the subjunctive for the contrary to fact statement *If the president were a woman*. C and D say *like* instead of *such as*. A and C aren't idiomatic; they say *marked with* instead of *marked by*.

## Drill 2

1. **D**. Should be: or a family.

2. **A**. In this day and time is redundant. Better to say: Today.

3. **B**. Should be: asked Bob and me.

4. **A**. misplaced modifier. Anita Hill was speaking before the committee, not her demeanor.

5. **C**. this list is: inflamed, forced, and caused.

## Drill 3

1. Since he kept breaking out in hives, Boris decided to go to a doctor...(*Being as* is never right; idiom)

2. ...looking intently at the road ahead, playing his radio at ear-shattering volume, and scratching his ever-growing hives. (parallel construction)

3. Inspecting a particularly large and glowing hive on Boris's rear end, the doctor responded by laughing heartily. (misplaced modifier)

4. "...one must take steps to relieve the stress in one's life." Or: "...but when you break out in hives...you must take steps to relieve the stress in your life." (pronoun agreement)

5. "one of those men who are leading..." (subject-verb agreement)

6. "If I were you I'd read Sartre..." (subjunctive)

7. He shouted that he loved his life more than the doctor did. Or: loved his life more than he loved the doctor. (the last version doesn't make a whole lot of sense in context.) (faulty comparison)

8. ...to pick up the prescriptions. (diction)

9. The effect of Boris's visit...which had the surprising effect of curing his hives. (diction)

## QQ #33: Billy Wifflamoo, The Final Chapter

Billy had several more visits from the aliens. Sometimes they ate snacks on his Buick; sometimes they played music and danced. One alien in particular became Billy's friend. The alien taught Billy some good tricks: a foolproof method for shooting foul shots, a lip smacking recipe for tadpoles, and a way to make his eyes change color at will.

Later in life, Billy found himself married, with two small children, living in a peaceful suburb. He said that he couldn't be happier.

"You miss the aliens," said his wife one night, putting the children to bed.

She was right. His Buick had long ago gone to the scrap heap and the aliens, once his friends, did not appear anymore. Sometimes it made Billy sad, but he threw himself into his work as an accountant for a chain of dry cleaners, and occasionally he made a little money making bets on his foul-shooting. Although he lived a sedate, quiet life he always treasured the days of snacking with the aliens.

## Part 8: World Series

## QUIZ #1

1. roamed

2. from

3. are

4. whom

5. caused

## QUIZ #2

1. with

2. She

3. were

4. indifferent to

5. which

## QUIZ #3

1. **B** (misplaced modifier)

2. **D** (faulty comparison)

3. **C** (redundancy)

4. **D** (idiom)

5. **D** (diction)

## QUIZ #4

1. whom, herself

2. they

3. their

4. which

5. who, those

## QUIZ #5

1. Plural subjects go with plural verbs; singular subjects go with singular verbs.

2. A gerund ends in -*ing*. It's the present participle form of a verb, but it functions as a noun.

3. Adverbs modify verbs, adjectives, or other adverbs.

4. A collective noun is a group noun, such as committee, family, or jury. Collective nouns are always treated as singular, unless you mean to show differences or disagreement within the group.

5. The subjunctive is used in (1) contrary-to-fact statements and (2) *that* clauses of order, command, or recommendation.

## QUIZ #6

1. **A**. This is a faulty comparison.

2. **D**. A, B, and C say *One*, which doesn't agree with *you* that comes later in the sentence. E is passive (*have an avoidance*) and unidiomatic (*avoidance to*).

3. **B**. A and E are redundant (*reason...is because*). In C, *being that* is never correct. In D, the verb *are* doesn't agree with the subject *reason*.

4. **A**. When comparing nouns, use *like*.

5. **C**. A and B violate subject-verb agreement by saying *study... are*. D and E aren't idiomatic.

## QUIZ #7

1. The purpose of art is not to instruct, but to allow...

2. Serious political discussion is better left...

3. Correct as is.

4. Writers whom I consider...

5. Rather than comply with...

# QUIZ #8

1. **D**. parallel construction

2. **A**. faulty comparison

3. **H**. redundancy

4. **B**. pronoun agreement

5. **F**. misplaced modifier

# QUIZ #9

1. it is hoped

2. my

3. number

4. among

5. is

## QUIZ #10

1. Nouns, phrases, or clauses that make up a list must be in similar form. Also, when using seesaw conjunctions, elements on either side must be in similar form.

2. Use *fewer* for countable, individual items, such as pencils. Use *less* for quantities, such as mashed potatoes or sand.

3. Ambiguous means vague, unclear. Ambivalent means having strong opposing feelings, such as love and hate, about one thing.

4. Redundancy is needless repetition. *Again and again.*

5. First find the verb. Then ask yourself, who or what is doing this action?

## QUIZ #11

1. What are adverbs?

2. What are conjunctions?

3. What are nouns?

4. What are interjections?

5. What are prepositions?

# QUIZ #12

1. A

2. A

3. A

4. E

5. E

# QUIZ #13

1. Before eating, Mindy packed four items for her trip: a mouse-trap, a hairbrush, a mug in the shape of a duck and a canned ham.

2. Canned ham was Mindy's favorite food; she ate it at least once a day, usually washing it down with a root beer float.

3. "I can't wait to leave for Costa Rica!" shouted Mindy, clutching her guidebook under arm and doing a jig.

4. Costa Rica, which is west of Panama, is extremely moun-tainous; Mindy had packed hiking gear long with a couple of extra canned hams for emergencies on the trail.

5. Mindy said that it was entirely possible that her life could be saved by a canned ham, if she found herself lost in the rain-forest with no knowledge of which plants were edible.

## QUIZ #14

1. with

2. as

3. of

4. to

5. on, in

## QUIZ #15

1. **D**. What made his reelection unlikely? *The recession.* A, B, C, and E don't give the recession as the subject of *made*.

2. **C**. In A, *it* has no clear antecedent. B mangles *necessarily*, forcing it to modify *need* when the meaning is *unnecessary investment*. D is awkward and wordy. E starts out well, but fouls up the tense: *would be*, not *will be*.

3. **E**. What was without electricity and phone service? *Many towns.* A and B violate subject-verb agreement by saying many towns *was*. C has a major verb problem, *that being*, which isn't English. D is a little wordy and not as straight-forward as E. These phrase substitution questions mimic the GMAT, and on the GMAT, go with the simplest answer.

4. **A**. The comparison is whales feeding to sharks feeding, plural to plural, which gets rid of B and C. C, D, and E make the comparison using *like* or *unlike*, when it should use *as do*, because we are comparing an action: feeding.

5. **B**. The verb is recommend, followed by a *that* clause, which requires the subjunctive. A, C, D, and E don't use the subjunctive.

# QUIZ #16

1. *Affect* is not a noun unless you are talking about psychology. *Affect* as a verb means to influence. *Effect* as a verb means cause to happen.

2. Use *between* when you are talking about two things; use *among* for more than two things.

3. It's fine to begin a sentence with *because* as long as you also have an independent clause eventually. *Because* will introduce a subordinate clause, which can't stand alone.

4. *Compare to* shows difference and similarity; *compare with* primarily shows difference.

5. A clause has a subject and a verb; a phrase does not.

# QUIZ #17

1. nauseated

2. Like

3. lies

4. he

5. was

# QUIZ #18

1. (subject-verb agreement) One of the first things to find out... is the location

2. Correct as is.

3. (parallel construction) Among the reasons...were that she was bored, that she had no further chance...and that she had a better offer...

4. (misplaced modifier) Wandering aimlessly through the city, the writer witnessed several tragic events that she recorded in her notebook.

5. (pronoun case, redundancy, use of subjunctive) The boss sent a memo to Buffy and me, recommending that we be on time to work.

# QUIZ #19

1. What is a prepositional phrase?

2. What is a noun clause?

3. What is a participial phrase?

4. What is an adjective clause?

5. What is a gerund?

## QUIZ #20

1. Wanda is, millions dye

2. Frogs have, which are

3. food happens to be, season is

4. Buffy and her friends realized, they had forgotten

5. Driving is

## QUIZ #21

1. **D** (parallel construction)

2. **A** (misplaced modifier)

3. **A** (pronoun case)

4. **E**

5. **E**

## QUIZ #22

1. had

2. allusion

3. claim

4. of

5. its, it (referring to photograph)

## QUIZ #23

1. What is faulty comparison? (Winky...loves geraniums more than Zippy does)

2. What is a punctuation mistake? (or more specifically, using a semicolon instead of a comma: Zippy's favorite thing was socks, and he...)

3. What is redundancy? (cooperation together is redundant. Just say cooperate.)

4. What is diction? (never say irregardless)

5. What is a misplaced modifier? (Dragging his massive suitcase...Winky didn't see his passport, still laying on the table...)

## QUIZ #24

1. Use *lay* in place of *put*, when there is an indirect object. I *lie* down. I *lay* the snail on the rug.

2. *Bring* to the speaker, *take* away from the speaker. *Bring* that snail over here. *Take* that slimy thing with you.

3. An infinitive is the *to* form of the verb: to sneeze, to screw. If you place an adverb (or anything else) between the *to* and the verb, you are splitting the infinitive: to loudly sneeze, to slowly screw.

4. *Infer* means deduce. *Imply* mean hint. I put on my coat, trying to *imply* that I wanted to leave. I *inferred* from his tone that he was upset.

5. Use a hyphen if the adjective comes before the noun: a *well-oiled* machine. Don't use hyphen if the adjective follows the noun: The machine was *well oiled*.

## QUIZ #25

We can't obviously, give you an answer key for your original sentences. You might ask someone who knows grammar to look them over for you, or you might turn to the respective chapter and review, to see if you avoided the pitfalls.

## ERROR ANALYSIS

To help you see what areas you need work in, we've organized the question from the World Series by type. Circle the questions you got wrong; if there are several in any one category, Go Back And Review! (Q6:4 means Quiz #6, question 4.)

## PARALLEL CONSTRUCTION:

Q1:5; Q7:1; Q10:1; Q18:3; Q21:1; Q25:2

## MISPLACED MODIFIER:

Q3:1; Q8:1; Q8:5; Q18:4; Q21:2; Q25:4

## TENSE:

Q1:1; Q12:1; Q17:5; Q22:1

## SUBJECT-VERB AGREEMENT:

Q1:3; Q5:1; Q6:5; Q7:2; Q9:5; Q10:5; Q15:3; Q18:1; Q20:1, 2, 3, 4, 5; Q22:3; Q25:5

## REDUNDANCY:

Q3:3; Q6:3; Q8:3; Q23:3

## PRONOUNS:

Q1:4; Q2:2,5; Q4:1, 2, 3, 4, 5; Q6:2; Q7:3, 4; Q8:4; Q9:3;
Q15:1, 2; Q17:4; Q18:5; Q21:3

## IDIOM:

Q1:2; Q2:1; Q3:4; Q7:2,5; Q9:4; Q14:1, 2, 3, 4, 5; Q16:4; Q22:4

## FAULTY COMPARISON:

Q3:2; Q6:1; Q8:2; Q15:4; Q17:2; Q23:1; Q25:1

## MOOD/VOICE:

Q2:3; Q5:5; Q12:3; Q15:5

## DICTION:

Q2:4; Q3:5;  Q10:3; Q12:2; Q16:1; Q17:1; Q22:2; Q23:4;
Q24:1, 2, 4

## PARTS OF SPEECH:

Q5:2, 3, 4; Q11:1, 2, 3, 4, 5

## PARTS OF THE SENTENCE:

Q16:5; Q19:1, 2, 3, 4, 5

## PUNCTUATION:

Q13:1, 2, 3, 4, 5; Q23:2; Q24:5; Q25:5

# NOTES

# NOTES

# NOTES

# NOTES

**NOTES**

# NOTES

# NOTES